SECRETS OF THE LONE WOLF TRADER

By

Patrick Buchanan

Dedication

This book is dedicated to Abbey, the little cat with the heart and soul of a Tiger, with whom I got to spend over 10 years of life with. The beautiful, wild creature who couldn't care less about money. All he wanted was love (and treats). Abbey helped keep me sane for so many years, and his presence made even the worst days seem beautiful. Whenever as he was in my arms, everything was OK. He will be in my heart (and on my arm) forever.

TABLE OF CONTENTS

Introduction 1

Chapter 1: First Things First 4

Chapter 2: The Big Picture 16

Chapter 3: Hardware and Software 27

Chapter 4: The Set Up..36

Chapter 5: My Daily Routine 84

Chapter 6: The Proper Mindset...........................109

Chapter 7: What to Trade?..................................122

Chapter 8: The Process 147

Chapter 9: Entries..160

Chapter 10: Managing the Trade 184

Chapter 11: The Art of the Chart 203

Chapter 12: Exits 209

Chapter 13: The Game of Risk............................225

Chapter 14: Dealing With Losing 238

Chapter 15: Dealing With Winning......................243

Chapter 16: Going Big: How and When to Scale......246

Chapter 17: From Open to Close..........................253

Chapter 18: Putting it All Together 264

Chapter 19: Money Money Money 294

Chapter 20: Remember What's Truly Valuable 302

About the author 308

Introduction

*note: if you'd like to pair this book with my complete day trading video course, visit www.lonewolftradingclub.com

I remember when I quit my life as an employee to become a full-time day trader. The first thing my mom asked me was, *"Don't you think you'll get bored just working at home by yourself?"* I was actually astonished by that question—I thought she knew me better than that. I replied, *"I will NEVER get bored with making a six-figure income working 5 hours a week and not having to deal with a single person."*

That last part of the sentence—*not having to deal with a single person*—is one of the most beautiful and personally fulfilling things about having a day trading career. Sometimes when I make $1,000 in 30 minutes at the beginning of the day, I still have to pinch myself. It's amazing to realize that I did this ALL BY MYSELF… with no clients, no customers, no product or service to market. No office space, no overhead, no cold calling, no networking, no invoices to send, no co-workers, and most importantly… NO BOSS.

A computer, a fast internet connection, and my brain. That's literally ALL I NEED to not only survive, but thrive. By myself, on my own terms.

In today's society you CAN'T overestimate the importance of being self-sufficient. Think about it. Even if you like your job and your boss, unless your boss is immediate family you don't *really* have any job security. If you think your employer has your best interest at heart, go watch the 2003 documentary "The Corporation" and then see if you feel the same way afterwards. When you work at a company—ANY company—**you are a cog in a machine.**

If you are the cheapest/most reliable/most pleasant cog the company can find, perhaps you are safe, for now. But the second some bean-counting consultant decides the company could save money by replacing you, do you think your 'pleasant and easy to work with' demeanor will save you? And with each passing day, AI becomes more powerful... so if they don't get a younger/cheaper person to do your job, maybe they will just get a machine to do it.

I'd like to thank every boss who's ever fired me *(there have been a few)*, because every time I was fired it reinforced what I already knew about myself: just how little respect I have for most of what constitutes corporate America, how little I have in common with it, and how much I wanted to become a Trojan Horse. Rolling deep inside corporate America's guts and taking whatever I could from it... like a selfish Robin Hood, stealing from the rich and giving it to myself. And that's literally what I do now, every single day. I know—I'm not *actually* stealing from these companies as I fatten my bank account with each click of the mouse… but is sure it fun to think of it that way.

You've heard the phrase "success is the best revenge," right? Well, I've never actually sought *revenge* against anyone, but it does make me smile when I realize that everyone who's fired me over the course of my lifetime is probably still doing a job that they don't actually *love* doing. Meanwhile, here I am truly loving what I do to make my living. Trading isn't 'work' to me. I literally feel like I'm playing a game for an hour each morning. Sure, some days I lose… but *most* days I win. It's a game of strategy and wits. Me playing against the market.

I tried as hard as I could to fit into the corporate world for many years, but with each passing job it became obvious just how important it was for me to create my own reality, design my own life exactly as I want to live it, and then do whatever it took to build that life—so that's what I did.

If you're feeling stuck, unsatisfied or un-appreciated at your job, here's the good news: you *can* take the power out of your employer's hands, take control of your future and *actually live* how you want to live. I said goodbye to corporate office culture forever, and so can you. I'm going to show you exactly how I did it in this book, step-by-step. Are you ready to fire YOUR boss? I think I know the answer to that question. Let's go.

CHAPTER 1

First Things First

"Whether you think you can, or you think you can't – you're right." -Henry Ford

Stop and contemplate this quote for a minute. In my opinion, this is one of the truest statements ever made, not just relating to business but life in general. Of course there are caveats, and of course the *thinking* needs to be followed by *doing,* but at its core, this statement is 100% TRUE. Everything I've managed to accomplish, I've done so because I *believed* I could. Without self-belief, you have no chance.

So before you continue, get your mind right. I mean it. The information in this book will be confusing at first. The learning curve will be steep. The steps & processes I'm about to teach you will take some repetition before they start to sink in and feel natural. But TRUST ME. If you *believe* you can do it, *you will be able* to do it. You may be thinking to yourself, *"I'm not a numbers person"* or *"I don't know the first thing about financial stuff."* Guess what? That's perfectly OK, because I thought the exact same things myself when I was first learning how to trade.

I've had many dark nights of the soul after big losing days, when I'd lay in bed at night and think to myself, *"Can I really do this? Maybe I'm just not cut out for it."* If I had listened to that voice in my head years ago, I wouldn't be self-employed making a a six-figure income in 5 hours per week right now. I wouldn't have started my own business teaching people my trading strategy. And I wouldn't be writing this book.

I realize the title of this book is ambitious. You might be asking, *"Can I really make six-figures in just five hours per week? How do I do that?"* Yes, you *really* can… and I will show you exactly how to do it in this book. There is a LOT to learn, and much of what I'm about to explain won't make sense *(at first)*, but once you get the hang of the process and understand the strategy, making hundreds of dollars per day will become easier and easier as the days pass.

It's important to remember, this is not a 'get rich quick' activity. Nobody should expect to make $10,000 in one day while only risking $500, or expect to be a pro trader in 1 month. That type of thing is NOT realistic, and anyone who tells you their 'system' can do that for you is lying to you.

Here's what IS realistic. There are *(on average)* 252 trading days per year. If a person made $400 per day for 252 days, that amounts to $100,800. It is ABSOLUTELY possible to make $400 per day trading with a small account, even if you only have $2,000 in your account to start with.

I remember when I started trading—at first I said, *"If I can just make $100 per day, I'll be happy."* And then after I was making $100 per day consistently for a few months, I raised that goal to $200 per day. And then $400, $500, $1,000. I achieved each goal and then I raised it. Right now, I don't even have specific daily targets. It's just so easy that it almost feels like I'm stealing money.

Before we go any further, I should clarify a few things. I have never been a 'finance bro.' I've never idolized the fictitious Gordon Gekko or any of the flashy douchebags who emanate his vibe in real life. I didn't go to business school. Hell, I still don't even consider myself to be 'a businessman' even though this is how I make my money.

I'm a musician, artist and writer who happened to stumble upon ONE strategy to use in the stock market that works extremely well, and that's what inspired me to write this book—so I can share as much of what I know to other people who may have also dreamed about making money in the markets but thought they never could. Even if you don't consider yourself 'business savvy' you can do it, and it's not as hard you think it will be. If I can do it, you can too.

Everything I know about day trading is self-taught. I've read countless books about trading, and absorbed hundreds of hours of YouTube videos and online tutorials. I've watched every 'free training' seminar I could find online, and I've sat in on many different day trading rooms as they traded live. I've gathered crucial bits of information from all these places, and I've used that info to synthesize my own particular style of trading that works extremely well for me, and I'm confident it will work you too—as long as you follow my steps closely and do everything the right way.

My trading strategy is extremely simple and actually very basic. One of the most important points I need to make right off the bat is—when it comes to day trading, you DON'T need to be able to do *everything*… you only need to be able to do ONE THING well, with consistency. It reminds me of a quote by the legend Bruce Lee: *"I fear not the man who has practiced 10,000 kicks once, but I fear the man who has practiced one kick 10,000 times."*

I also need to make this crystal clear: my strategy relies 100% on **day trading stock options**. This is not investing, and it's not pure equity stock trading, It's day trading *stock options.* **What I'm going to cover in this book will be limited to the information you need to know in order to trade the way I do,** which is about 1% of the totality of what you *could* learn about the stock market & options trading.

Plenty of information about the market and day trading will be left out, and that's on purpose. This book is NOT meant to be a comprehensive options class, but rather an extremely detailed description of *exactly what I do* every day, to make myself between $500-$2,000 in approximately 30-60 minutes per day.

It's not all sunshine and rainbows. Like I said above, YES, there is a learning curve... and it's a pretty steep one at first. You WILL feel overwhelmed, I guarantee it. But I *also* guarantee you, if you just stick with it, you will experience numerous 'lightbulb moments' when you realize that a concept which seemed incomprehensible just a few weeks ago suddenly makes sense—the moment when the chart doesn't look like a prehistoric hieroglyph anymore, but rather a pattern that you can actually decipher.

Once you do get the hang of it and you're actually making hundreds of dollars a day for doing very little work *(I don't even consider it 'work' at all)* you may wonder if you're living in a dream. I can't tell you how many times I've made $600-700 in 15-20 minutes. As a matter of fact, as I type this at 8:58AM, I just closed my last position on AMD for a profit of over 11% on the day. Not bad making 11% on your money in 25 minutes.

Back when things were just starting to click for me and I'd have days like this, I'd think to myself, *"Did that really just happen?"* YES. Yes it really did just happen, and it wasn't due to luck. It was due to the skills I had developed. You can develop these exact same skills, and you might even be able to develop them quicker than I did… but that all depends on YOU.

THE WAY OF THE WOLF

I've structured this book in chronological order, starting at the beginning & working through all the different aspects of real-life day trading, in the order in which I feel is most beneficial to the beginning trader. We'll go through some real-life examples of trades that I took, and I'll explain exactly why I took them, when I got in, how I managed it and when I exited. There will be plenty of photos to cross reference, so you'll be able to follow along visually in order to make more sense of it. Even if you have NO experience whatsoever, I'm going to teach you all of the essentials that you'll need to know in order to trade the same way I do.

And if you *do* already have some trading experience, I'm sure you'll be able to benefit from seeing a different approach. Maybe you've been trading a different style & want to try your hand at trend trading. Maybe you've been spinning your wheels and want a fresh look. Maybe you're tired of trading penny stocks that are woefully unpredictable.

Wherever you're at in your journey, I'm confident you'll find some useful information in this book. If you're an intermediate to advanced trader, you can skip ahead to chapter 9 if you'd like—that's when I get into explaining the specifics of my entries with examples of how & why I do what I do. For everyone else, please read through each chapter in chronological order, because that will give you the best chance for success.

Throughout the book, whenever you see something you don't understand as you're reading—I would urge you to put the book down and do more online research into that specific topic. I realize there's a MASSIVE amount of information relating to the market *in total*, so if I were to attempt to write the 'comprehensive day trading options manual' that book would be thousands of pages long. I'm not trying to do that. I'm sure there will be times when you'll read something here and think, *"I wish he had gone into further detail about that."* There is *always* further detail to be found online about *anything...* so don't hesitate to put the book down, do outside research as needed, and come back when you're ready.

My main goal with this book is to explain my entire day-trading process with as much detail as I can, but without including any unnecessary information. I want to give you all the info you need, and nothing you don't need. My strategy is not complicated, but just because it's not complicated doesn't mean it's basic. You'll see what I mean by the time we're finished.

If you start to feel overwhelmed as we dive head-first into the seemingly endless rabbit holes that exist in the world of day trading, remember this— although there are a million things you *could* learn about… you don't need to learn everything about everything. In fact, with my strategy you only need to learn a *fraction* of what constitutes the totality of the market.

Think about it like this: if you're planning a cross-country road trip from point A to point B and you open up a map, you'll see millions of places you *could* go along the way, from giant metropolitan cities to tiny towns. And there will be so many different ways to get to all of those different cities or towns. But the thing is, you only need to go to ONE place, and you only need to take one particular route *(usually the fastest one)*. This is a good analogy to my style of trading. I'm taking the fastest, most direct route to get from Point A *(my trading account)* to Point B *(my trading account, now with more money in it)*.

 To utilize my trading strategy, you don't need to know anything about the Greeks, or selling naked puts, or complicated plays like Iron Condors, Strangles and Straddles- all you need to learn are the basics: interpreting candlesticks and candlestick patterns, identifying support & resistance levels, knowing the difference between buying puts and calls, strike prices and contract expiration dates…

and more importantly, how to see the charts as ART rather than just data. that's about it.

If I had to explain my trading strategy in a single sentence, it would be this:

I use a specific combination of candlesticks, time frames and indicators on my charts to identify emerging trends, join the trends as they develop by buying call or put options, then take profits before the trends reverse.

This is the simplest and easiest way to make consistent profits, period. Back when I was first starting out, I experimented with 'contrarian trading' concepts, meaning: I'd attempt to pick tops and bottoms of moves and get in right *before* the reversal happens. So for example, if the stock is pushing up, I'm trying to go short by identifying the perfect time to get in, right *before* a huge wash happens. This style is no doubt very exciting, because there's an adrenaline rush you'll feel when you're right and a huge reversal happens 1 minute after you get in with your contrarian position. I can't lie: it's a super cool feeling when that happens.

That's why I totally understand the allure of wanting to feel like you're able to 'predict the future.' The problem is, you'll end up being wrong more often than you'll be right. And WHY would want to take on the extra risk of attempting to predict the future when the actual, REAL direction of the stock trend is right in front of your face, right NOW?

Sometimes I think people have a hard time believing it actually IS this simple. It's like they've been scared off by so much talk of how hard this is, or how risky this is, etc. Yeah, it CAN be hard and risky, but it doesn't *need* to be. With the strategy I've developed, I've been able to take out much of the complexity and the inherent risk involved, because we're joining moves that are *already in progress* instead of attempting to predict the future. You don't need to wonder *if* or *when* a move is about to happen... it's already happening, and we just profit from it while it's still going strong. As soon as it starts to weaken, we get out with our profits.

One of the things that's unique about my strategy is the particular way I combine different types of candlesticks, time frames and indicators into a 'big picture' view that gives me a high percentage chance of identifying when trends begin and end. You'll never be able to capture the entirety of a move, but the more of the move you DO capture, the more money you'll make.

If you're just flailing around trying a bunch of different approaches, trading as if you're throwing everything at the wall to see what sticks, then you're doomed to fail. You need to focus on trading ONE specific way, and then sticking to that way and refining the process. Don't get hypnotized by the latest & greatest shiny new objects. Don't go chasing a bunch of random penny stocks that some online 'guru' claims are heading to the moon. Do one thing, and do that one thing VERY well, with consistency.

Trying to learn everything there is to know about the stock market is virtually impossible. Imagine standing in the middle of a forest and being required to identify every detail of every tree you see—you would immediately be overwhelmed. But if you were only required to focus on identifying the details of ONE tree while ignoring the rest—*that* is doable. We are going to focus on that 'one tree' *(metaphorically speaking),* and we're not going to bother with the million other trees in the forest.

Here's another analogy: imagine the greatest podiatrist in the world. This doctor knows everything there is to know about feet, but might not have the slightest idea of how to do brain surgery. Likewise, the greatest brain surgeon in the world may have a very limited knowledge of feet. Both are brilliant doctors, but brilliant in very distinct specialties.

This concept is relatable to the stock market. The fact that there are endless tickers you *could* trade, and so many different ways you *could* trade all of those tickers—this fact alone gives a lot of people the dreaded 'paralysis by analysis' feeling. This paralyzing feeling of having too much information is what keeps a lot of people from entering the market in the first place, and it's also what makes people take a lot of silly, random trades that they shouldn't have taken.

I want to re-iterate— this ISN'T an 'Options 101' book. Over the last few years I've developed and fine-tuned a specific strategy that relies on a particular combination of candlesticks, time frames and indicators in order to work. I'd rather spend our time teaching you everything about *my particular* setup, trading style and strategy, rather than just doing a 'basics' course with a lot of material that you can find elsewhere.

There is beauty in simplicity, and I believe that my strategy is one of the simplest, easiest to understand strategies out there. How do I know it works? Because I've personally made well over six-figures per year doing exactly what I'm abut to teach you. That's how I know it works. So without further ado, let's get into it.

CHAPTER 2

The Big Picture

"**Keep your face always toward the sunshine—and shadows will fall behind you.**"—Walt Whitman

So how will we make six figures working 5 hours per week? We'll do it by **DAY TRADING STOCK OPTIONS.**

In the simplest terms: **day trading stock options involves the buying and selling of options contracts within a single trading day**, meaning—we will open AND close our positions in the same day. This makes day trading MUCH different than *investing*, which always involves parking your money somewhere for a much longer period of time. Day trading is like your daily driver car, and investing is like the '63 Corvette Stingray you have parked in your garage... the one you rarely ever drive.

In case you're wondering what options are: **Options are financial derivatives that provide the right** (*but not the obligation*) **to buy or sell an underlying asset, such as stocks, at a predetermined price** (*the strike price*) **on or before a specific date** (*the expiration date*). Day traders capitalize on short-term price movements in these options to make profits.

So what does this mean in layman's terms? It means that if you buy a CALL option, you have the right to buy the stock at a certain price *(which is the strike price)*. If the price of that underlying stock goes UP, then you can sell that option for a profit. Traders profit when the options they control give them a cost advantage over the market price for that underlying stock. The same thing goes *(but in reverse)* if you have bought a PUT option.

In the simplest terms: if you buy CALL options, you make money as the stock's price rises. If you buy PUT options, you make money as the stock's price falls.

But remember there's also timing involved—you might be GREEN on your option at 10AM, but if the price suddenly reverses on you, you might be RED at 10:15. That's why it's VERY important to develop your skill with entering and exiting your positions at the right time. The way to do this effectively is what constitutes the bulk of the information in this book.

DAILY OPERATION

Here's a very simplified example of how an options trade works:

Let's say you buy a call option on a particular stock *(this goes for any stock or ETF)* at the $100 strike price, because based on your technical analysis you believe the price of the underlying stock will rise within the next hour. You end up being right and the price of the stock *does* rise. 20 minutes later you believe the stock price doesn't have much more room to increase right now *(the upwards trend is running out of steam)*, so you decide to close the position *(sell that same contract you bought 20 minutes earlier)* At this point, the options contract you just sold will be worth more than it was worth when you bought it 20 minutes earlier. The exact same thing would be true *(but in reverse)* if you had bought a PUT option instead, thinking that the price would drop—and then the price *did* drop.

There's no standardized, specific amount that the price of an options contract always rises or falls. That depends on many factors, like market volatility, options premium, the price of the underlying stock, the amount of time until expiration, etc. But we're not concerned with all of that yet. We'll get there.

At the *absolute* basic level, this is how I trade:

I BUY CALLS WHEN I EXPECT THE PRICE OF A STOCK TO RISE

I BUY PUTS WHEN I EXPECT THE PRICE OF A STOCK TO FALL

There are a LOT of other plays you *could* make regarding options, and you can find plenty of services that will talk about Iron Condors or selling put credit spreads or any other number of plays, but ALL I DO IS BUY CALLS OR BUY PUTS. That's it. Whether I decide to buy put or call options of a specific stock is determined by many different factors which we'll get into as the book progresses.

Stock prices can do one of three things throughout the day:

- RISE *(move up)*

- FALL *(move down)*

- CONSOLIDATE *(move sideways)*

It is possible to make money when price is moving sideways all day long, but the tactics you'd need to use in order to profit in these conditions are NOT part of my strategy. I only buy calls or puts, therefore I only want to see upwards or downwards trending price action *(depending on if I'm long or short)*. Sideways price action is the kiss of death to the way I trade—it's like trying to drive a motorcycle that's in neutral.

Another key aspect to my strategy is getting in and out quick to take advantage of the added volatility in the morning session. Added volatility creates larger price fluctuations as the stock pushes up or down during the first 30-60 minutes of the day. Yes, it IS possible to make money holding a position throughout the day, but this is less predictable, more time consuming, and therefore not as ideal as opening *and* closing the position within the first 30 minutes to 1 hour of the trading day.

Below are some important basic concepts. Don't worry if some of these seem confusing right now. It will all make a lot more sense once I explain how this works *during the process* of trading.

- Call and Put Options: There are the two main types of options—call options and put options. There are more variations you could buy/sell… but like I said, ALL I DO is buy calls or buy puts. A call option gives the holder the right to buy the underlying asset at the strike price, while a put option gives the holder the right to sell the underlying asset at the strike price.

- Choosing the Underlying Asset: In day trading stock options, the 'underlying asset' is typically a stock or an exchange-traded fund (ETF). Traders choose options based on a few different factors, including their expectation of the underlying asset's price movement and the price of the option itself. I trade mainly SPY, QQQ, AAPL, AMD, META and a handful of other stocks. The ticker symbols for a stock can be used interchangeably with the phrase 'underlying asset.'

- Selecting an Options Contract: Options contracts have standardized expiration dates and strike prices. Before you open a trade, you'll need to choose the specific expiration date for that contract. Since my strategy involves opening & closing trades on the same day *(day trading)*, my strategy uses short term expiration dates *(the nearest-term weekly expiration date)* SPY and QQQ each have same-day expirations, which I do NOT like—I want to have at least one full day before expiration so that the option premium doesn't 'melt down' too quickly on me. That 'price meltdown' is known as Theta decay *(or time decay)*. We'll touch on this later on when I'm actually taking you through a trade.

- Risk Management: Day trading is volatile, so risk management is crucial. You should only risk a small percentage of your total account size on each trade to protect yourself from significant losses. Exactly how much per day *(or per trade)* you should risk is something you'll need to determine for yourself. Like with many things in trading, you'll need to strike a balance. If you don't risk anything, it's VERY hard to make any serious profits. Likewise, if you're always risking 100% of your account with every trade, it's more likely you'll 'blow up' your account *(lose all of your capital).* I'll take a deep-dive into the concepts & strategies of risk management in chapter 13.

- Technical Analysis: My strategy relies heavily on using technical analysis to identify support & resistance levels, and using certain indicators that act as support or resistance levels. This is how I identify short-term price trends and entry/exit points. I study various chart patterns, moving averages, and specific technical indicators to help me decide which stocks to trade each day, and when to enter/exit the trade.

- Volatility Considerations: Volatility affects option prices. Higher volatility generally leads to higher option prices, and vice versa. This is one reason I prefer to trade first thing in the morning when the market opens. The most volatility of the day occurs within the first 30-60 minutes of the day, and while some people deliberately avoid this volatility, my strategy actually takes advantage of volatility to produce even bigger profits. This is also why I tend to trade smaller size on Fridays, because there's usually less volatility on Fridays than during other days of the week.

And here's some basic terminology you should understand:

- Long Position: When we buy a CALL option, we do so because we expect that the price of the underlying stock will rise *(that's why we bought a CALL and not a PUT)*. Doing this gives us a *long* position.

- Short Position: This is the opposite of a long position. When we buy a PUT option, we do so because we expect that the price of the underlying stock will fall *(that's why we bought a PUT and not a CALL)*. Doing this gives us a *short* position.

- Bid: The highest price at which a buyer is currently willing to purchase a security or option.

- Ask (or Offer): The lowest price at which a seller is currently willing to sell a security or option.

- Bid-Ask Spread: The difference between the highest price a buyer is willing to pay *(bid)* and the lowest price a seller is willing to accept *(ask)*. This represents the transaction cost of executing a trade.

- Market Order: An order to buy or sell a security at the best available price in the market at that moment. Market orders are executed immediately. **I ONLY USE MARKET ORDERS** when I trade. Why? Because the options I trade have lots of liquidity, meaning: anyone can enter or exit their position quickly without much slippage *(a wide bid-ask spread)*.

- Limit Order: An order to buy or sell the option at a specific price. This type of order will only be executed if the market reaches the specified price or better. This will assure that you get filled at the exact price you want, but it also means you could lose your opportunity to get into a position quickly. Time is money, and that's why I never use limit orders. I'd rather know I'll get into the trade immediately once I hit the 'buy' button.

- Stop Order (Stop-Loss Order): An order placed to buy or sell a security once it reaches a certain price level. It's used to limit potential losses or protect profits. This type of order can be useful if you aren't able to closely monitor your trades *(due to scheduling conflicts, work, etc.)* and you want to protect yourself from large losses if the trade goes against you.

- Day Order: An order that is valid only for the current trading day. If it is not executed by the end of the trading day, it will be canceled.

- GTC (Good 'Til Cancelled) Order: An order that remains in effect until it is either executed or canceled by the trader.

- Volatility: The degree of variation in the price of a security or market over time. Higher volatility indicates greater price fluctuations.

- Liquidity: The ease with which a security can be bought or sold without significantly affecting its price. High liquidity means there are many buyers and sellers, making it easy to execute trades. All of the tickers I trade have a high level of liquidity.

- Margin: Borrowed money from a brokerage firm to finance trading positions. Margin allows traders to control larger positions with a smaller amount of capital, but it also increases risk. I trade with a cash account, so margin doesn't play any part in my trading style. If you DO plan on using margin in your trades, it's very important that you get educated on this topic. Since I never use margin when I trade, I'm not going to get into that topic in this book.

- Day Trader: A trader who opens and closes positions within the same trading day, with no overnight exposure to the market. This is what we do every day. DAY TRADING.

- Pattern Day Trader (PDT): In the United States, a pattern day trader is one who executes four or more day trades in a five-business-day period using a margin account. PDTs are subject to specific regulations and account requirements, UNLESS you trade with a cash account, and this is the reason I trade with a cash account.

These are just a few of the many terms used in day trading. It's easy to find a lot more information online relating to all of these terms, so if there's anything you'd like to learn more about just put the book down, go do some research elsewhere, then come back after you've studied up!

CHAPTER 3

Hardware and Software

"He who knows that enough is enough will always have enough." — Lao Tzu

What do you need to start trading? **A computer, a fast internet connection, an external monitor and your trading software.** There, we're finished with this chapter.

But seriously, that really *is* all you need.

If you're reading this book now, chances are you've done enough research about the stock market to see plenty of photos of day traders posing triumphantly in front of a wall of monitors, looking like air-traffic controllers poised to land some planes. You might be asking yourself, *"Do I need a wall of monitors to be a successful trader like this nerd?"* Nope. You don't need that. You need **ONE** external monitor. Although I'm currently using 2 monitors, you only *need* one.

But before we even dive into the hardware & software, I want to talk about the actual space you'll be in as you trade—both physically and mentally. It should go without saying that having a separate office space is ideal... but you'd be amazed at how many people think it's totally fine to set up the laptop at the end of their kitchen countertop and trade while toasting a bagel at the same time. Don't be that person. Take it seriously. This is *(or can be)* your *actual job*, so treat the entire process with the respect it deserves.

If you don't have a dedicated office, you should at least have a dedicated trading area set up somewhere in your house or apartment that's *not* your bedroom. You don't want to co-mingle the energies of trading and sleeping in the same area, as they are polar opposites. If you assign the mental imprint of all the excitement, fear, joy and anguish you'll experience trading to the same place you sleep, you might have a harder time sleeping. It's much better to set up a small desk in the corner of your living room or dining room—anywhere else *besides* your bedroom is fine. But of course, a home office is always the ideal situation.

I use a standing desk, and I love it. I find that standing up as I trade really keeps me focused, alert, locked into exactly what I'm doing from open to close. I'm not allowed the luxury of slouching down in a comfy chair and daydreaming, and if I happen to have any nervous energy it's easy to step back & forth instead of keeping that energy all bottled up in a sitting posture. Last but not least, the health benefits of standing desks are proven, and I believe keeping the mind/body connection healthy and balanced is extremely important.

Let's talk about the mind for a minute. One of the things that's often overlooked is the importance of stopping to assess your own state of mind before trading. Less than favorable life events happen to everyone, and we're not always in a good headspace. If you've just had a breakup, or some other personal drama, or you're hungover, or you got 3 hours of sleep last night, don't trade. There's a great reason why surgeons and airline pilots can't show up to work hungover.

But if you absolutely *must* trade for whatever reason, scale back your size considerably. If you're mentally compromised or just not 'locked in' and focused, trade with smaller size. If you normally trade 20 contracts per day, just trade 3-5 that day. If you normally trade 5 contracts, just trade 1. You always want to give yourself the best odds of winning in every way, and trading while you're mentally less than 100% is doing the opposite of that.

OK, back to tech talk. Your main desktop *(or laptop)* screen will be used to view your 15 minute & 30 minute charts, and your external monitor will be used to view your 1 minute charts. We'll get into exactly how to setup your screens in the next chapter. The external monitor is really where the magic happens— this is where you keep your eyes focused most of the time. The 1-minute chart is the most important one we'll be looking at, even though all of them are valuable and each plays an integral part in combining information.

When people ask me, *"How fast should my computer be?"* My response is always, *"The fastest computer you can afford."* And that's absolutely true. You *should* buy the fastest computer you can afford—but that doesn't mean you *can't* trade with a budget computer. For years I made money using the cheapest MacBook Air you could buy.

Honestly, the processing power of your computer has less of an effect on your success than a fast, reliable internet connection does. Having blazing fast internet speed is THE most important part of trading success. So if I had the choice between getting a top of the line computer and average internet speed or an average computer with maximum internet speed, I'll choose option 2 every day of the week.

The LAST thing you want is to hit that 'buy' or 'sell' button at a certain price, and then have your order lag because of slow internet speed…and by the time your order fills the price has changed drastically. That SUCKS. Even a 2 second delay can make a huge difference in the fill you get. When you click that button, you want the order to process IMMEDIATELY.

About the external monitor—as with the computer, you should buy the best monitor you can afford. But again… you *can* have success with a budget monitor. Like with my laptop, for years I traded on the cheapest external monitor you could buy… $79 at Walmart *(can you tell I wasn't born rich?)* That budget monitor did a perfectly acceptable job of displaying my charts and giving me all of the visual feedback I needed.

I use the very first external monitor I owned as my second monitor now, arranged on the right side of my laptop. You certainly don't need 2 external monitors—just one. If you can see your charts clearly, that's really all you need. We're not doing online gaming here. You don't need a 360Hz refresh rate.

And last but not least, you'll need your trading software. There are a lot of different options available, some are paid and some are free. I suggest you do some online research and draw your own conclusions as to the pros & cons of each one.

I recommend using TD Ameritrade's Think or Swim (TOS) because that's what I'm using *(it's also free to get, but each options trade will cost you .65 per contract)*.

There are some *completely* free alternatives *(no charge at all to trade options contracts)* so if that's something that's important to you, there are other ways to go. But beware: is anything in business ever *truly* free? Although a brokerage like Robinhood will give you commission-free trades, it comes at the cost of limitations elsewhere. It's up to you to do your research and discover the pros and cons of every possibility.

If you want to get your screens set up *exactly* like mine, and make sense of each photo in this book, I recommend using TOS. You'll just open an account with TD Ameritrade *(make sure it's a CASH ACCOUNT to avoid the PDT rule... more on that in a minute)* then you'll deposit some money into it *(which you will use as your trading capital)* and then you'll download the Think Or Swim desktop app on your computer.

I'm not going to lie—Think Or Swim has a fairly steep learning curve, but once you realize that you only need to pay attention to a fraction of the things on the screen it will be a lot easier than it looks at first.

If you're already using other trading software, you can still benefit from the strategy and concepts in this book— just take these concepts and apply them to the software you already know. But if you're a beginning trader, just do yourself a favor and get TOS to make the process as easy as possible for yourself.

As I mentioned above, be sure to get yourself a CASH account in order to avoid the PDT rule. So just *what is* the PDT rule?

The Pattern Day Trader (PDT) rule is a regulation imposed by the U.S. Securities and Exchange Commission (SEC) on traders who engage in day trading activities with margin accounts. A pattern day trader is defined as someone who executes four or more day trades within a five-business-day period using a margin account. A 'day trade' is defined as the buying and selling or short-selling and covering of the same security on the same day.

We are DEFINITELY going to be completing more than four day trades per week, so we most certainly do NOT want to get flagged with the PDT rule, and that's why we trade with a cash account.

PDT Rule Activation:

Once a trader executes four or more day trades within a five-business-day period, they are designated as a pattern day trader by their brokerage. Once labeled a pattern day trader, the trader is subject to the PDT rule's restrictions, which are:

- Pattern day traders are required to maintain a minimum account equity of $25,000 in their margin account on any trading day.

- If the account equity falls below $25,000, the trader is prohibited from making any day trades until the account is brought back above the minimum requirement.

Consequences of Violating the PDT Rule:

If a pattern day trader executes day trades while having less than $25,000 in their account, they might face restrictions from their brokerage, such as trading limitations and potential account suspension. Brokers are also required to issue a 'Day Trade Call' to the trader, notifying them of their violation and the need to deposit additional funds to meet the $25,000 requirement.

Alternative Accounts:

If a trader does not meet the $25,000 minimum requirement, they can still engage in day trading activities using a cash account. However, cash accounts have their own limitations, such as the requirement to wait for settled funds before trading and no access to leverage.

LONG STORY SHORT: **If you are starting out with LESS than 25K in your account** (*as most of you are*) **and you plan**

on making more than 4 trades per week *(which ALL of you should be doing)* just get a cash account, and your problems are solved.

You'll only be able to trade with cash you actually have, and then at the end of each day your profits or losses go from 'unsettled cash' to 'settled cash,' and then you start out fresh the next day with your new total amount of capital in your account. If you're doing everything right then that total amount should be bigger each day than it was the day before.

Chapter 4

The Set Up

"Give me six hours to chop down a tree and I will spend the first four sharpening the axe." — Abraham Lincoln

Now that you have your computer *(laptop or desktop)* and your monitor, it's time to actually install your trading software. As I mentioned in the last chapter, there are a handful of perfectly capable trading platforms you can use, each with their own visual layout & idiosyncrasies, so it all comes down to personal preference.

If you want to copy my *exact* screen setup, you'll need to use TD Ameritrade's Think or Swim platform since that's what I'm using. It's always been reliable for me, and my orders have always been executed quickly. There have only been a handful of times out of 1,000's of trades that I've experienced any lag, so I really don't have any complaints about it.

There's really no such thing as THE best trading software *(that all depends on what features are most important to you)*. Traders of all skill levels use a wide variety of programs like TradingView, Webull, Interactive Brokers, Fidelity,

Lightspeed and more. Different platforms have different strengths and weaknesses. All of them allow you to look at charts and place trades, and ultimately that's all you really need. I'm only telling you to use TOS so that when I'm explaining how to arrange your screens a certain way, use certain indicators, etc., you will be able to have *your* screen look *exactly* how mine looks.

One thing I highly recommend: once you do choose your main 'go-to' trading software, stick with it and take a deep-dive into learning everything you can about *that* particular platform. Although the visual basics of reading a chart and identifying candlestick patterns will translate into any trading software, it will be much more beneficial to you to really learn *one* platform in depth rather than dip your toes into multiple platforms.

The last bit of prep you'll need to do: whatever trading software you're using, **make sure to set ALL of your preferences to their most robust settings, allowing the software to work as fast as possible and use the maximum amount of CPU from your computer.**

For example, on TOS there's a system setting option that allows you to change whether you have 'real time' *(no delay)* quotes, or whether you want a delay on the quote speed. Obviously, you want NO delay. Everything that you can customize in the software should be set to maximum speed, maximum power for the software. Delays ALWAYS mean less accurate info for you.

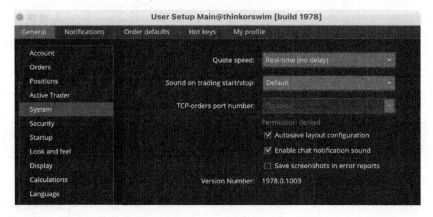

The first time you fire up your trading software and look at the main screen it will be completely overwhelming. I know, because that's exactly how I felt. In the beginning I said to myself, *"There's NO fucking way I'll be able to make sense of anything on this screen."* The feeling was so strong I almost gave up before I began.

The screen looked like it came straight from a dystopian science fiction movie, like something an evil genius would use while attempting to destroy the planet. It took me a while to get used to it, and it will probably take you a while as well. And that's OK! There's nothing 'time sensitive' here. You can take as long as you need to feel comfortable. And after you set up your screens the way I have mine arranged, you can follow along with everything in this book step-by-step. Remember, you are doing this on your own time frame. If you're ready to go in a week that's great… but even if it takes months, no big deal—you'll get there when you get there. it's better to be truly *ready* to trade than it is to rush into things.

As you view the many numbers, graphs and visuals on your screen, it will ease your mind to remember this: a *lot* of what you'll see on a chart is inconsequential information, and you don't need to pay any attention to it. I'll make sure to let you what what you DO and DON'T need to focus on. The overwhelming feeling you'll have when you first look at your main screen will soon disappear as you realize you only need to focus on a very small amount of what you actually see on the screen.

A piece of housekeeping before we start dissecting the charts: in real life, when you're looking at the candles on your screens they will appear as RED or GREEEN candlesticks. Since the photos in this book are printed in Black and White, just remember that the RED candles will appear in the book as the darker looking candles, while GREEN candles are the lighter of the two.

Also, bullish *(upwards trending)* patterns are made up of mainly GREEN candles, and bearish *(downwards trending)* patterns are made up of mainly RED candles. So when you're looking at the photos and my caption says something like, *"See the big red candle after the two green candles?"* You're looking for the *darker* candle after the two *lighter* candles.

Now that you have your computer, monitor, and trading software opened up, *where* are you actually going to look, and *what* are you going to focus on as you decide what to trade?

MAIN MONITOR

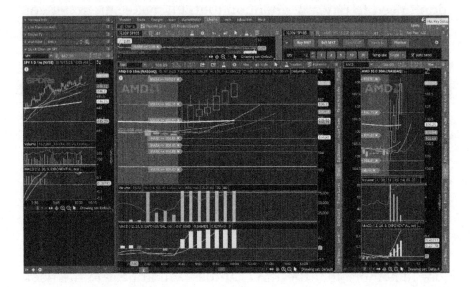

One of the cool things about TOS is that you can customize your workspace *(called 'grids')* to include as many different boxes as you'd like to see onscreen at the same time, and each of those boxes can contain any number of charts or indicators. You can save multiple grids to use for different purposes. I have my daily go-to grid titled 'main', which is the one you see in the photo above. I also have one titled

'naked' which is just one box taking up the entire
that's useful when I only want to focus on one timefran..
view it large.

I have a third grid titled 'travel' that I use if I'm traveling and
don't have my external monitor but still want to trade. It's a
modified version of the main grid, with the 2 boxes being a 1-
minute regular candlestick chart next to a 30 minute Heiken
Ashi candlestick chart—that gives me the immediate price
action but also lets me see the longer intraday trends
developing.

Once you become skilled, you can experiment and make your
own grids to see if you find anything that works even better
for you. You could have as many individual boxes as you'd
like visible at once—but It's very difficult to interpret a lot of
information on one screen, and that's why I keep my screen
limited to 2 charts per grid.

LEFT HAND VERTICAL COLUMN

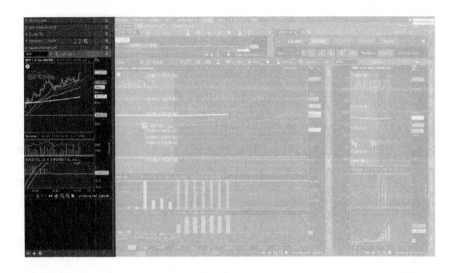

You can see on the left hand side we have one vertical column, which contains what TOS calls 'gadgets.' You can add as many gadgets as you'd like here, but obviously if you added 20 gadgets you won't be able to have all of them open at the same time due to screen real estate. If you want to add gadgets, simply click on the little PLUS symbol at the bottom left, and a menu will pop up showing you all of the possibilities. You can also change the width of the column by hovering over the divider bar on the right side of the column and then dragging it until you have your preferred width.

The only gadget you can't delete from this column is 'account info.' You can see that in addition to account info, I have added live news, trader TV, watchlist, and a quick chart which I have set to the 1-minute time frame. You can set this quick chart to show any ticker or time frame. Usually, I am viewing QQQ or SPY in this chart because QQQ and SPY are the ETF's whose price movement gives you a good sense of the 'big picture' movements for the day.

The only 2 gadgets that I consider 'essential' in the left hand column are watchlist and quick chart: watchlist because I have it linked to my BUY/SELL buttons, so that I can execute orders quickly, and quick chart so that I can quickly see how the QQQ or SPY is moving when I want to cross reference price action of a stock ticker to one of these ETF's.

The only time I use live news is if I want to read the latest news articles about a particular stock, and trader TV can be set to watch live financial news broadcasts like CNBC, the Schwab network, and others. The only time I really pay attention to this is when there's a fed announcement I want to watch live, or if some major event happens and I want to see breaking news. Other than those situations, I usually leave trader TV off, because it's better to stay focused and pay attention to your charts.

A bit more about how/why my watchlist is connected to the BUY/SELL chart: although you won't be able to identify the color coding here since the photo is printed in B&W, you will see the outlined number "9" next to the top 3 boxes across my screen. You will also see the outlined number "1" on the two boxes in the main window of the screen *(the 15 and 30 minute charts).* If you click the drop down menu on these numbers, you'll see it can be set to 'unlink' or the numbers 1-9, with each number corresponding to a color-code. The specific number you use to link your boxes together makes no difference.

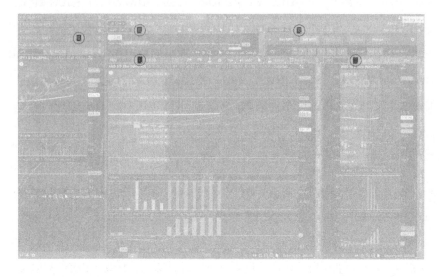

What IS important is this: all of the boxes on your screen that are linked together will change when you change the ticker of *one* of these boxes. Why is this important? Because if you have a number of orders ready to go in your watchlist and you have your WATCHLIST linked to your BUY/SELL window, then any order you click on in the watchlist box will be 'live' in the BUY/SELL box, ready to be executed with a single click of the mouse.

So, for example—let's say you have a handful of different orders prepared and waiting to be executed in your watchlist window. One of your orders is a META put. You're watching the META chart, ready to pounce once you see the right signals telling you to go short. When you DO see those signals telling you it's time to execute, you simply need to click that META put order in the watchlist, and *that particular order* is the one that will populate and be 'live' in the BUY/SELL box. Now, when you fill in your desired number of contracts and hit the big green BUY MKT button, you will immediately buy that number of META put contracts. And here's what this actually looks like on your screen:

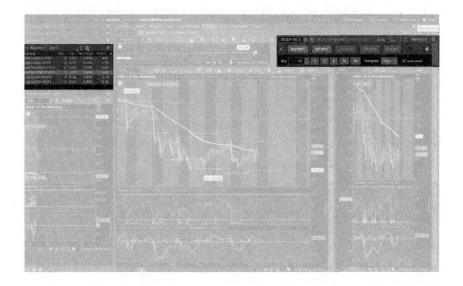

In the image above, I've highlighted the WATCHLIST and the BUY/SELL screen, which are linked to each other *(in this*

case, they are linked by the number '9'). First, look at the box on the left, which is the watchlist. We can see six different options orders loaded into our watchlist, including puts *and* calls for AMD, META and QQQ.

The specific order that's highlighted says **META230922P302.5**. Moving from left to right, here's what this info means: The underlying stock for this option is **META**. '**230922**' means that the expiration date for this options order is September 22, 2023. And '**P302.5**' means that this is a PUT option at the strike price of 302.5. On the right side of the order we see the number 6.05. This means that each contract we buy will cost *approximately* $605.

Now jump over to the box on the right side. This is the BUY/SELL order box that's linked to our watchlist. You should always have the Template drop down menu set to 'Single' and you should always have the 'auto send' button checked *(this means there's no additional screen that pops up before your order is placed)*. Notice that in the 'Qty' box it says 3. This means we're set to buy 3 contracts. The '1,3,5,10,20' numbers here are templates, but you can also use the +/- buttons or just type in the exact number of contracts you want to use.

So now, the second we hit the 'Buy MKT' button, we will instantly purchase 3 of the META230922P302.5 options contracts highlighted in the watchlist, and it will cost us approximately $1,815. And if we selected the top order in the watchlist, AMD230922C100, *that* specific order would immediately be 'live' in the BUY/SELL box *(since our 2 boxes are linked)...* so if we clicked that top order and then hit 'buy' we would purchase 3 CALL option contracts of AMD at a 100 strike price for $301 per contract.

You can see how powerful this is in real-life trading situations, because you can have multiple trades all set up and ready to go—you can have put AND call options ready to go on a bunch of different tickers, and different strike prices—all of them are 'locked and loaded' so-to-speak. If you set alerts on multiple tickers at multiple long or short levels, then when a specific alert goes off you can click that specific order in your watchlist, then hit 'Buy MKT' and you're in the trade immediately.

The other *(much less effective)* method is to watch price action, then when you want to execute you go to the options chain and look at the right expiration date and strike price, *then* click the 'buy' button... and then a drop down menu will come up asking you to confirm your order, and then after you confirm that you will have placed the trade. This second way of doing things will take you at least 1 minute longer to complete than my preferred way of doing it. Sometimes price can make HUGE moves in just one minute, so obviously the quicker you actually DO get into the trade once you decide to pull the trigger, the better off you'll be.

MAIN WINDOW

As I said above, you can have as many different boxes as you'd like on your grid, and you can resize each window as you see fit. In the main screen image we just discussed, notice the little graphic to the right of the words 'Main' and 'Hot Key Setup' in the top right corner. It shows 4 small boxes. This means I've set up my main window to be populated by 4 boxes, the two smaller ones at the top *(which are linked together with number 9)* and the two larger ones at the bottom *(which are linked together with number 1).* I personally feel that trying to interpret more than 2 charts on one screen gets very convoluted and confusing *(trust me, I've tried it)...* so I keep my main screen view limited to 2 charts at once.

You *could* assign a number of different things to each box, like Level 2, big buttons, times and sales, active trader, etc. I don't want you to worry about any of that, because we won't use any of that. The only thing you'll need is a regular old candlestick chart inside each box.

On this main window I have my 15 minute Heiken Ashi chart larger in the middle of the screen, and my 30 minute Heiken Ashi chart on the right side, smaller. Why is the 30 minute chart smaller? Because we're dealing with a longer time frame, so the trend is easier to spot with less bars.

If we look at a 1-minute chart and we're only able to view five red candlesticks together, we can't determine with any certainty if there's actually a bearish trend happening. Sure, all five candlesticks are red and price is obviously falling, but they're *one minute* candlesticks. Price might have been steadily rising all day, and it's just having a tiny pullback in that 5 minute range that we're focusing on before it makes the next push higher.

But if we see five large red candlesticks together on the one hour chart, that's obviously a bearish trend, and shows us that price has basically been falling for the entire day. Perspective matters, and you'll need to zoom out on your 1 minute charts to see more of 'the big picture' in order to interpret what's actually happening.

CANDLE POWER

Now is probably a good time to start getting into the nuance of candlesticks, since they are the bread & butter of trading. They are the pasta in the Italian meal, they are the engine in the race car…. you get the picture. Without candlesticks, there is no effective trading. Sure, you *could* just look at numbers and make your play based off of that information…

but WHY would anyone want to do that? Candlesticks are the visual representation of price action.

In my strategy, I use 2 different types of candles: the standard Japanese candle for the 1 minute chart *(and the 5 minute chart whenever I pull that one up)*, and Heiken Ashi candles to view the 15 and 30 minute charts. During my morning pre-market preparation, I use the standard candle to view the daily chart and plot our support and resistance lines.

Occasionally I'll look at shorter time frames with Heiken Ashi candlesticks just to get a different perspective, but my basic strategy uses the Japanese candlesticks for shorter time frames. Why the Japanese candlesticks for 15 minutes or less, and Heiken Ashi candlesticks for 15 minutes or more? Let's take a look at some differences between them, and the reason will become clear.

The Japanese Candlestick

In Japanese candlestick charts, each candlestick represents the open, high, low, and close prices of a specific time period, such as a minute, hour, day, etc. I have mine set to the standard colors of red for downward price action and green for upward price action. The color of the candlestick indicates whether the closing price is lower or higher than the opening price. Japanese candlesticks provide a clear view of the price action and show the relationship between open, high, low, and close prices for each period. Patterns like doji, hammer, shooting star, and engulfing patterns are more easily recognizable on Japanese candlestick charts.

The MOST important reason to use Japanese candlesticks on the 1-minute time frame chart is because it shows the most immediate, real-time price action, with no lag or smoothing effect. And REAL TIME price action is what you want when you're entering and exiting a position.

Heikin Ashi Candlestick

Heikin Ashi candlesticks are designed to provide a smoother representation of price trends by averaging out price data. The open price of a Heikin Ashi candlestick is the average of the previous candle's open and close prices. The close price is the average of the open, high, low, and close prices of the current period. The high and low prices are modified to reflect the actual high and low for that period, but smoothed to some extent. Heikin Ashi candlesticks are normally color-coded in the traditional Red or Green colors to distinguish between bullish and bearish candles.

Because of the smoothing effect, **Heikin Ashi charts can make trends and reversals easier to identify,** reducing the impact of short-term noise and volatility.

And *that's* the main reason I like to view 15 minute or less charts using Japanese candlesticks, and 15 minutes or more with Heiken Ashi charts. The combination of both types of candlesticks allows me to see the immediate, untouched price action on the 1 minute chart with Japanese candlesticks *and* identify longer-term intraday trends more easily due to the smoothed-out color coding of the Heikin Ashi charts.

It's extremely easy to see the visual difference between looking at a Japanese candlestick pattern and a Heiken Ashi candlestick pattern. Do this exercise to see for yourself: Pull up any ticker's 1-minute chart and look at the entire day using Japanese candlesticks. Now look at the exact same chart, but use Heiken Ashi candlesticks instead. You'll immediately see what I mean.

In a nutshell: Japanese candlestick charts provide a more detailed, immediate representation of price action, making it perfect for entries and exits—while Heikin Ashi candlestick charts offer a smoother representation that makes it easier to identify trends. I *could* trade with only one type of candlestick if I had to *(just like I can successfully trade with no external monitor when I have to)* but having both types of candlesticks to view just makes life easier. And don't you want to make life easier?

TURN UP THE VOLUME

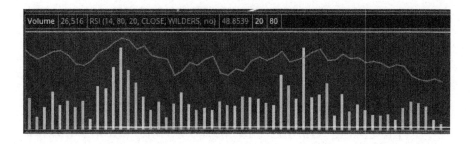

Volume is one of the most deceptively important aspects of trading when it comes to 'seeing the big picture' of price action and trend formation. At first glance, volume just looks like little red & green bars at the bottom of the screen. But volume represents the total number of shares, contracts, or units traded during a given period, making it an extremely important tool when day trading.

Here are a few reasons why Volume is significant:

- Confirmation of Price Movements: Volume can confirm the validity of price movements. When the price of a stock moves in a certain direction with high volume, it suggests strong market participation and increases the likelihood that the price movement is significant. This is a bit like having one friend tell you how great a new movie is as opposed to 100 friends telling you how great that movie is. You'll probably feel more confident the movie will be great if every person you know tells you so. More volume=more market participation=more validity.

- Trend Validation: Volume helps confirm the strength of a trend. In an uptrend, rising prices accompanied by increasing volume can signal strong buying interest and validate the upward movement. Similarly, a downtrend accompanied by higher volume indicates stronger selling pressure.

- Reversal Signals: Sudden changes in volume can signal potential trend reversals. An increase in volume during a price reversal suggests a potential shift in market sentiment and can serve as an early warning sign for traders. If you see a potential reversal that has very low volume on each candle, that's less valid than a potential reversal accompanied by large volume on each candle. Basically, when you confirm a potential reversal with volume, you can more easily avoid fake reversals. And this dovetails nicely into the next point:

- Avoiding False Signals: Low-volume price movements can result in false signals. I like to see price movements accompanied by sufficient volume to ensure the move is not merely a result of low participation. Volume often provides a level of confirmation that a price move is 'real' and not a quick fake-out *(unfortunately, fake outs happen often in the market).*

- Breakouts and Breakdowns: High volume often accompanies breakouts *(when price moves above a resistance level)* and breakdowns *(when price moves below a support level.)* High volume during these moves adds credibility to the breakout or breakdown.

- Liquidity Assessment: Volume provides insight into the liquidity of a security. Higher volume generally means greater liquidity, making it easier to enter or exit trades without significant price slippage. This is important since I use market orders. Having more liquidity means less slippage *(difference between the bid price and the ask price)* which is obviously good for me.

- Divergence Analysis: Volume divergence occurs when the direction of price movement does not match the direction of volume. Bullish divergence happens when prices decline but volume decreases less or starts increasing, potentially indicating an upcoming price reversal. Bearish divergence occurs when prices rise but volume decreases or starts increasing less.

- Exhaustion and Climax Points: Extremely high volume can signal exhaustion or climax points. Such points often indicate that a trend or price movement might be reaching an extreme and could soon reverse.

- Confirmation with Indicators: Volume can be used in conjunction with technical indicators to provide confirmation or divergence signals. For example, volume combined with an oscillator like the Relative Strength Index (RSI) can provide more reliable signals. I have my RSI overlayed on top of my volume chart so that I can see the combined view of the RSI with volume. You *could* combine any number of indicators on the same graph, but this usually doesn't work for me. I'd rather have less information to look at and make the connections myself rather than be overloaded with visual information. Putting the RSI on top of the Volume bars is one of the few instances where I stack indicators.

- News and Events: Important news releases, earnings reports, or other market-moving events are often associated with high volume. Monitoring volume during these events can help you make successful trades during periods of heightened volatility. I honestly hate it when any type of scandalous or unexpected news events happen, because that introduces a great deal of unpredictability into trading. For everything else in life, I love unpredictability—it keeps things interesting. But in trading, I want everything as predictable as it can possibly get.

ALL ABOUT INDICATORS

So the first thing you notice when you look at your trading software are the big red & green candlesticks making all of those patterns on the screen. Then you'll probably notice the volume chart below that. We've just covered all of that.

The next thing you'll notice is all the other *stuff* on your screen...the stuff that makes your screen look like it belongs in the air traffic controller room of an international airport.

One of the most popular questions beginning traders have and one I get asked frequently: *"How many indicators should I have on my charts?"*

Here's the short answer: SIX. That's it. Here they are.

1. **200 EMA**

2. **Williams Alligator**

3. **50 EMA**

4. **MACD**

5. **RSI**

6. **Daily High/Low**

These six indicators are all you need to give you the best chance of winning with my strategy, and the first three on the list are essentially the same type of indicator (exponential moving averages), just set up with different time frames. We put 4 indicators on our candlestick chart *(the 200 EMA, the Alligator, the 50 EMA and the daily High/ Low)*, we overlay the RSI on our Volume bars, we put the MACD at the bottom. Done!

I should notice 2 'honorable mention' indicators that I don't have on my charts 100% of the time, but I frequently check if I'm trying to get additional confirmation or if I'm looking for levels where price could bounce: These two indicators are the Keltner Channels and Pivot Points.

Remember, when it comes to indicators, more is NOT better. There are literally hundreds of indicators you *could* use on your trading software, but you only need the five listed here. Don't think about indicators as a predictor of what will happen—your own ability to analyze a chart and read the movement of the candlesticks is how you 'predict the future.' Indicators are simply a way to give you reassurance and extra confidence that you're about to make the right trade before you pull the trigger, and let you know when it's time to enter or exit a trade.

Here's more detail on the indicators I use:

200 EMA (exponential moving average)

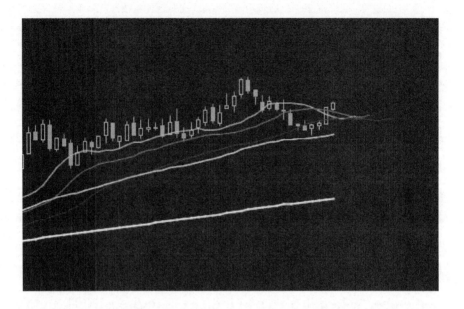

In the image above we can see the three indicators that I overlay on my candlestick charts, the 200 EMA, the 50 EMA and the Alligator Indicator *(the daily high/low is on this chart too, but it's out of the frame in this image).* The other indicators I use *(MACD and RSI)* are below the main candlestick chart. The MACD gets it's own space, and as I mentioned before—I overlay the RSI on the Volume bars.

In the example image above, you can see that the indicators are 'stacked' in a bullish way, with price and Alligator above the 50 EMA, which is above the 200 EMA *(the thickest white line at the bottom).* You can also see how everything is trending bullish by the upwards slope of the line. It's ideal to see our indicators stacked like this. The direction doesn't always need to be bullish—it can move either upwards *or* downwards, and whether it's stacked bullish or bearish will simply determine whether we go long or short.

The 200-day Exponential Moving Average (EMA) is a widely used technical indicator. Pretty much every trader agrees that the 200 EMA always represents a significant price level. It's a moving average that calculates the average price of a stock over the past 200 trading days, giving more weight to recent prices. The EMA is a type of moving average that reacts more quickly to recent price changes compared to the Simple Moving Average (SMA), which gives equal weight to all data points.

So how does the 200-day EMA work?

- Calculation: The 200-day EMA is calculated by taking the sum of the closing prices of a stock over the past 200 trading days and then dividing it by 200. However, it gives more weight to recent prices, which means that the latest prices have a larger impact on the calculation than older prices. I like EMA's more than SMA's because what's happened recently is more important than what's happened 3 months ago, so the recency bias of the EMA works in our favor here.

- Trend Identification: The 200-day EMA is often used to identify the overall trend direction of a stock or the broader market. When the stock's price is above the

200-day EMA, it is often considered to be in an uptrend. Conversely, when the price is below the 200-day EMA, it's seen as being in a downtrend. This is a key aspect of my strategy since I trade the trend—usually I will only go long when price is trending upwards on the 1-minute chart *above* the 200 EMA, and only go short when price is trending downwards *below* the 200 EMA.

- Support and Resistance: The 200-day EMA can also act as a support level during uptrends and as a resistance level during downtrends. I always pay close attention when the stock price sits near the 200-day EMA to gauge potential reversals or trend continuations. The 200 EMA often acts as a 'tipping point' when price crosses above or below—I will frequently act on this fact when I'm trading.

- Long-Term Trend Confirmation: If a stock is trading above the 200-day EMA, it's generally seen as more bullish and might indicate a healthier, sustained trend. Likewise, when it's continually trading below the 200 EMA, this is a bearish trend. Simply following the trends is the heart of my strategy, so of course I pay very close attention to the way price action relates to the 200 EMA on a daily basis.

- Market Timing: A bullish crossover *(50-day EMA crossing above the 200-day EMA)* might indicate the potential for an uptrend, while a bearish crossover *(50-day EMA crossing below the 200-day EMA)* might indicate the potential for a downtrend. The relationship between these 2 EMA's can provide valuable signals, so I always pay close attention to how they're reacting to each other on an intraday basis.

WILLIAMS ALLIGATOR

The Williams Alligator indicator was developed by trader and author Bill Williams. It's designed to help identify trending and ranging markets, as well as potential entry and exit points within those trends. The indicator uses a combination of three moving averages on different time frames *(the default setting is 13 period, 8 period, and 5 period, but all three are customizable. I leave mine on the default settings.)*

My absolute favorite thing about this indicator is the easy to understand visual feedback it provides. You can instantly tell the direction and strength of a trend *(or the lack of a trend)* simply by noticing the degree of the slope of the lines, and the relationship of the spacing between the three moving averages. As the line spacing gets wider, the trend is getting stronger. As the lines grow closer together, we have less trend *(or a consolidation phase)*. Also, the differentiating colors of each line makes immediate visual recognition of the trend very simple.

The three moving averages of the Alligator indicator are named after the Alligator's mouth: the 'Jaw' *(blue)*, the 'Teeth' *(red)*, and the 'Lips' *(green)*. Here's how the indicator works:

- Jaw (Blue Line): The Jaw is the slowest moving average and typically has the longest period. This line signifies the long-term trend direction. When the Jaw is pointing upward, it suggests a bullish trend. Conversely, when the Jaw is pointing downward, it suggests a bearish trend.

- Teeth (Red Line): The Teeth is a medium-speed moving average with a shorter period than the Jaw. It helps traders confirm the trend and provides a mid-term perspective. When the Teeth line crosses above the Jaw line, it suggests a potential bullish signal. Conversely, when the Teeth line crosses below the Jaw line, it suggests a potential bearish signal.

- Lips (Green Line): The Lips is the fastest moving average with the shortest period. It provides a short-term perspective on price movement. When the Lips line crosses above the other lines, it indicates a potential bullish signal. When it crosses below the other lines, it indicates a potential bearish signal.

As I just said, one of the best things about the Alligator indicator is the way you can easily see the strength of a trend, based on the spacing and directionality of the three moving averages. Here are a few key signals the indicator can provide:

- Alligator Awakening (Buy Signal): This occurs when the three lines start diverging, with the Lips moving upward above the Teeth and the Teeth moving above the Jaw. It suggests the potential start of an uptrend and a buying opportunity.

- Alligator Sleeping (Sell Signal): This happens when the three lines start converging, with the Lips moving downward below the Teeth and the Teeth moving below the Jaw. It suggests the potential start of a downtrend and a selling opportunity.

- Alligator Eating (No Clear Trend): When the three lines are intertwined and moving closely together, it indicates a lack of clear trend. As I've said before (and will say again) consolidation is NOT my friend. I like to stay out of the market when I'm not seeing a well defined trend.

In the image below we see an EXTREMELY bearish chart on AAPL. In fact, this intraday 1-minute chart is 100% bearish. Everything is obviously trending bearish, and continues that way for about an hour until price bounces and starts a trend reversal, which you can see in the lower right hand side of the image. You literally *cannot* find any extra confirmation *(based on the strategy & indicators I use)*. The highlighted oval area where price hits the jaw of the Alligator as a resistance level and then rejects would be the perfect place to go short.

I'm getting a bit ahead of myself here, because I'm touching on some things that will be explained in greater detail later on in the book... but I just wanted to give you a picture of what an OBVIOUS trend looks like. This short trade would be a no-brainer to get into, but things are rarely this simple.

Usually, it takes a bit more work to identify strong trends with conviction.

It's important to note that the Williams Alligator indicator can generate false signals, especially in choppy or ranging markets. Therefore, like any technical indicator, it's more effective when used in conjunction with other indicators to give you more confirmation. Remember: confirmation is key. I'll repeat that over and over in this book, because it's IMPORTANT. Never jump into a trade simply because you see something develop on one indicator. In the example above, it's 100% obvious this is a strong bearish trend, so if you see something like this develop on the charts, you can take that trade with confidence.

MACD

The Moving Average Convergence Divergence (MACD) is a popular technical indicator used to analyze trends, momentum, and potential buy or sell signals. It's based on the relationship between two EMA's, and is designed to help traders identify changes in momentum and potential trend reversals. I love using the MACD because like the Alligator, it identifies trends with quick and easy to understand visual feedback.

Here's how the MACD indicator works, and its key components:

- MACD Line (Fast Line): The MACD line is calculated by subtracting the 26-period EMA from the 12-period EMA. The resulting value represents the difference between the shorter-term and longer-term moving averages. The MACD line moves above and below a zero line, which represents the equilibrium point between the two EMAs.

- Signal Line (Slow Line): The signal line is a 9-period EMA of the MACD line. It helps smooth out the MACD line's fluctuations and provides a more stable reading of the indicator's trend.

- Histogram: The histogram is the visual representation of the difference between the MACD line and the signal line. When the MACD line crosses above the signal line, the histogram turns positive. Conversely, when the MACD line crosses below the signal line, the histogram turns negative.

The main uses of the MACD indicator are:

- Trend Identification: The MACD indicator helps us identify the direction and strength of a trend. When the MACD line is above the zero line, it suggests an uptrend, and when it's below the zero line, it suggests a downtrend.

- Momentum Analysis: The convergence and divergence between the MACD line and the signal line provides insight into the momentum of the trend. A widening gap between the two lines indicates increasing momentum, while a narrowing gap suggests a potential reversal.

- Crossovers: MACD crossovers are commonly used as trading signals. A bullish crossover occurs when the MACD line crosses above the signal line, indicating a potential buy signal. A bearish crossover occurs when the MACD line crosses below the signal line, suggesting a potential sell signal.

- Divergence: MACD divergence occurs when the MACD indicator's direction disagrees with the direction of the price trend. Bullish divergence happens when the price makes lower lows while the MACD makes higher lows. Bearish divergence occurs when the price makes higher highs while the MACD makes lower highs. Divergence can signal potential trend reversals.

RSI

The Relative Strength Index (RSI) is a commonly used momentum oscillator in technical analysis that helps us assess the strength and potential reversals of price trends. The RSI measures the magnitude of recent price changes to evaluate overbought and oversold conditions. It ranges from 0 to 100 and is typically plotted as a line graph. The RSI can take up its own space on your charts if you'd like, but I overlay it on top of the Volume bars. A lot of indicators don't really 'play nice' with each other, but I find that Volume + RSI is a combination that works well visually in the same space.

Here's how the RSI indicator works and its key components:

- Calculation: The RSI is calculated using the average of upward price movements *(gains)* and the average of downward price movements *(losses)* over a specified lookback period *(usually 14 periods)*. The RSI equation can be expressed as: RSI = 100 - (100 / (1 + RS)), where RS *(Relative Strength)* is the ratio of average gains to average losses.

- Overbought and Oversold Levels: The RSI is typically displayed on a scale of 0 to 100. It has two main reference levels: Overbought *(usually set around 70)*: When the RSI rises above this level, it suggests that the asset might be overbought, and a price reversal or correction could be imminent. Oversold *(usually set around 30)*: When the RSI falls below this level, it suggests that the asset might be oversold, and a price reversal or bounce could be near.

- Divergence: RSI divergence occurs when the direction of the RSI doesn't match the direction of the price trend. Bullish divergence happens when the RSI forms higher lows while the price forms lower lows, indicating a potential price reversal to the upside. Bearish divergence occurs when the RSI forms lower highs while the price forms higher highs, suggesting a potential reversal to the downside.

- Signal Generation: RSI crossovers of the overbought and oversold levels can be used as potential trading signals. However, traders often wait for the RSI to cross back into the normal range *(between 30 and 70)* before acting on the signal to avoid false signals during strong trends.

The main uses of the RSI indicator are:

- Momentum Assessment: RSI helps traders gauge the strength of the current price trend. High RSI values might indicate strong upward momentum, while low RSI values might suggest strong downward momentum.

- Overbought and Oversold Conditions: RSI helps identify potentially overbought or oversold conditions, which can occur when the levels cross above or below your upper + lower limit settings.

- Confirmation: RSI readings can be used to confirm price trends. For example, in a bullish trend, higher RSI values might support the continuation of the uptrend, and vise-versa with lower RSI values in a bearish trend.

One thing I should mention about my RSI settings: I've been 'faked out' too many times by false overbought/oversold signals that can happen with the default 70/30 setting—and that's why I use an 80/20 setting. Now, whenever the price falls below the 20 level or above the 80 level, I'm much less likely to bite on a false signal. When it's above 80 or below 20, a reversal is much more likely to be *real.*

DAILY HIGH/LOW

The Daily High/Low Indicator, also known as the Daily High/Low Range Indicator, is a simple technical analysis tool used to display the difference between the highest and lowest prices of a stock over a specific time period. I set mine to 1 trading day. This indicator gives me a visual reference of where the current price is at any given time relative to the previous day's calculation.

Here's how the Daily High/Low Indicator works:

- Calculation: The calculation is straightforward. It subtracts the lowest price *(the daily low)* from the highest price *(the daily high)* over the chosen time frame, which is typically one trading day.

- Interpretation: The resulting value of the Daily High/Low Indicator represents the price range that the asset covered during the trading day. A larger range indicates higher volatility and potentially more significant price fluctuations during the day. A smaller range suggests lower volatility and relatively stable price movement.

Although this is the simplest indicator on the list, it's extremely useful as a quick visual reference of a support or resistance level I can use to determine whether a trend is strong or weak. For example, if price has been trending up for the day and it bumps up against the previous day's upper level of the High/Low indicator—if it effortlessly breaks through that level, it's just one more piece of information to confirm that the bullish trend is strong. But if the price hits the pervious day's upper level, stalls and starts to reverse, it could mean the bullish trend is not that strong. Now remember, this doesn't guarantee there's going to be a big reversal and price will suddenly plummet. There is very little 'if/then' in trading. It's usually 'if/probably.'

Remember, each piece of information you gain from an indicator needs to be compared with other pieces of information in order to get a more complete picture of what's happening. Never make your trading decisions based solely from *any* one indicator or any one piece of information. Always combine all of the information you receive from multiple sources to see the big picture.

KELTNER CHANNELS

The Keltner Channels is one of my 'extra' indicators I frequently check, even though I don't keep it on my charts 100% of the time. It's named after its creator, Chester W. Keltner *(what a name)*, and it's used to assess volatility and potential price trends. The Keltner Channels consists of three lines plotted around the price chart: an Exponential Moving

Average line, an upper channel line, and a lower channel line.

Here's how the Keltner Channels indicator works and its components:

Exponential Moving Average (EMA):

The EMA serves as a baseline trend indicator and provides insights into the overall price direction. The centerline of the Keltner Channels is usually a 20-period Exponential Moving Average of the asset's price, but **I set my centerline to a 50-period EMA rather than the default 20-period EMA.** This gives me a smoother visualization of recent price action.

When you change the EMA line from 20 the 50 the visual feedback of the line won't look as responsive, but I prefer the smoother look of the 50 EMA to the 20 EMA, and this also gives me the tried-and-true 50 EMA/200 EMA crossover view with just 2 indicators. The less visual clutter I see on my screen, the better it is for me.

- Upper Channel Line: The upper channel line is calculated by adding a multiple of the Average True Range (ATR) to the EMA. The ATR measures market volatility over a specific period. Adding a multiple of ATR to the EMA creates an upper boundary that expands during more volatile periods.

- Lower Channel Line: The lower channel line is calculated by subtracting a multiple of the ATR from the EMA. This creates a lower boundary that narrows during less volatile periods.

The main purposes of the Keltner Channels are:

- Volatility Assessment: The width between the upper and lower channel lines gives an indication of market volatility. Wider channels suggest higher volatility, while narrower channels indicate lower volatility.

- Overbought and Oversold Conditions: Similar to Bollinger Bands, the Keltner Channels can be used to identify potential overbought or oversold conditions. When the price moves above the upper channel line, it might suggest overbought conditions. Conversely, when the price moves below the lower channel line, it might suggest oversold conditions.

I like the way that the spacing between the three lines gives me an immediate visual representation of the volatility of current price action. For pure trend identification I still prefer the Alligator with the 50 + 200 EMA's, but I do like checking the Keltner Channels to gauge volatility.

WHY MORE INFORMATION IS NOT ALWAYS BETTER

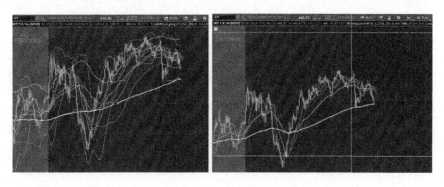

Take a look at these two charts side by side. The one on the left has a lot of popular indicators added to it, and the one on the right is the one I use daily, with only the Alligator indicator, 50 EMA and 200 EMA added. Look at the difference in the amount of visual information on the screen. On my setup, it's easy to see the up or down movement in price action. It's easy to spot when price crosses above or below the 50 or 200 EMA. You can easily spot where the candlesticks sit in relation to the other indicators on the screen. And if I wanted to assess the volatility at any moment, I'd just hide the Alligator and check the Keltner Channels.

Now look at the chart with all of the added indicators overlayed. This is the same chart, and these 2 screenshots were taken just minutes apart. Do you see how much harder it is to actually confirm a definitive direction of the price action? Suddenly, the big, white 200 EMA doesn't jump off

SECRETS OF THE LONE WOLF TRADER

the screen as quickly as it did before. The huge red and green candles are the only places where it's possible to detect any trend. This chart looks like it was created by Jackson Pollock.

Usually more information is better, right? I'm reminded of those old sayings, *"The more you know"* and *"Knowledge is power."* In *most* cases that's true… the more information you can collect, the better off you'll be… but not here.

We need to make split-second decisions as we enter and exit. If you're looking at MY chart setup, you can immediately see if price action is trending, up, down or sideways. You can immediately tell whether price is ABOVE or BELOW the 200 EMA. Putting a dozen indicators on your charts will make you second guess yourself. You'll look at the convoluted mess of lines and think, *"This indicator makes it look like it's going up, but that one makes it look like it's falling."*

Another problem I have with adding too many indicators to your charts is that in your attempt to uncover the truth, you're actually clouding the truth. By slapping a million different indicators on your charts in an attempt to predict the future, you're just obfuscating the truth of the price action that's right there on your screen.

You don't need to try to 'uncover' where price will be an hour from now… you can see where price IS, *right now*, no crystal ball needed. Just be aware and tuned into the candlesticks and the patterns you're seeing on the charts, and react to that. *YOU* are the determining factor in your success or failure, not the indicators you add to your charts.

OK! Now that we're all caught up on the basics of candlesticks, chart types and indicators, we can get into how and why I have my screens arranged the way I do.

MY MONITOR SETUP

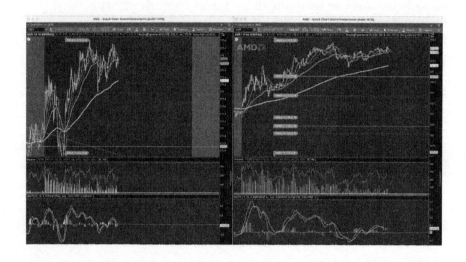

Here's how I have the charts arranged on my external monitor. I keep 2 charts up, centered so that one fills the left side while the other fills the right side of the monitor. In the example above I have the 1-minute QQQ chart on the left side and the 1-minute AMD chart on the right side, but *specifically* which charts I have up on each will frequently change from day to day. Usually I'll keep either QQQ or SPY up on one of the charts, because these 2 ETF's provide a picture of the 'overall' direction of the day.

What I mean is: if both SPY and QQQ's are ripping, it's a pretty good bet that most of the tickers I trade will also have a green day *(and vice-vera if SPY and QQQ are both falling hard).* I usually avoid diverging on the SPY & QQQ. Of course, sometimes both SPY and QQQ will go one way and a particular stock will go the other, but usually blue-chip stocks follow these ETF's general direction on the day.

And here's what my laptop *(or desktop)* screen looks like.

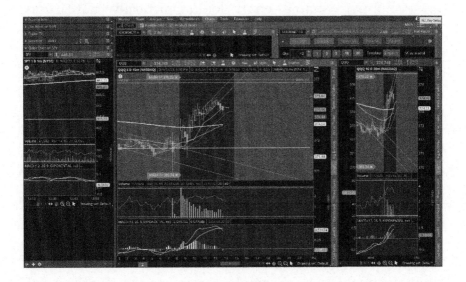

You can see that I have the largest box in the center of the screen set to the 15 minute Heiken Ashi candles and then the smaller box on the right is set to the 30 minute Heiken Ashi chart. On the left side we can see the vertical column that is populated with gadgets, and below the main chart windows we see the volume chart with the RSI overlayed, and the MACD below that. And that's it. No extra information needed.

One last thing to mention: you can customize the view you'll on your charts, both vertically and horizontally by zooming in or out on either axis. You could make a chart that's basically consolidating look a LOT more active simply by increasing the vertical zoom. Likewise, you could make a very choppy, volatile chart look practically flat if you drastically decreased the vertical zoom level.

So what I'm saying is: your eyes can play tricks on you depending on how you have the zoom set on your charts. Perspective is everything, so make sure you're not too zoomed in or out on either axis. You'll want to be able to see enough of the chart to get a decent 'big picture' view, but you don't want to be *so* zoomed out that you can't pick up small details of the candlestick movements.

So to summarize—with this exact setup, I'm able to simultaneously view a single ticker on the 1 minute, 15 minute and 30 minute charts, with different views *(Japanese candlesticks for 1 minute, Heiken Ashi for 15 and 30 minutes)*, and I'm able to see all of my indicators on every chart. And by linking my watchlist to my BUY/SELL box, I'm able to enter and exit my positions with lightning speed. I consider this to be a "goldilocks" type of visual setup, since I have *enough* information to give me confidence, but not *so much* information that my head is swimming with too many possibilities.

Now, that you're all set up, let's break down my daily routine.

CHAPTER 5

My Daily Routine

"It's the repetition of affirmations that leads to belief. And once that belief becomes a deep conviction, things begin to happen." —Muhammad Ali

THE DAILY PROCESS

So what does the actual step-by-step process of day trading look like? I'm normally trading in the Central time zone of the US, so for me the market opens at 8:30AM every morning. I feel sorry for my friends on the West Coast who need to wake up before 6AM... but some people actually *like* getting up that early. One advantage of living on PST time is that if you need to keep an actual day job with 'normal' office hours then you can trade the first hour of the day and still make it to work on time *(well, maybe not if you have LA traffic to deal with...)*

Here's what my weekdays look like *before* the market opens:

1. Wake up at 8AM

2. Make coffee

3. Fire up the trading machine

4. Study the pre-market action on all of my potential tickers for the day *(usually SPY, META, AMD, QQQ and AAPL)* and pay attention to any price gaps or trends that have developed after-hours/premarket

5. Study the daily chart action on those same tickers

6. Interpret the connection between the pre-market action and the daily chart

7. Place alerts at key levels of support & resistance that I'll use to determine when to enter a trade.

8. Ask myself the question, *"How much money will I make today?"*

9. Wait for the opening bell and start trading

I want to elaborate on a few key steps of my pre-market routine.

Step 4: Study the pre-market action

"Pay attention to any price gaps." So what exactly are gaps? Gaps in the stock market occur when the price of a stock opens significantly higher or lower than its previous day's closing price, resulting in a visible gap on the price chart. It's very rare that the market will open *exactly* where it closed. A 'flat open' is when price opens very near *(but not necessarily exactly)* where it closed the day before. When price opens

with a gap up or down, whether the gap gets filled or continues to run in the same direction of the gap largely depends on the type of gap and the broader market conditions.

There are four main types of gaps:

- Common Gap: Common gaps are often the result of normal market fluctuations and are not typically driven by significant news or events. These gaps have a higher chance of getting filled relatively quickly. As trading resumes, the price tends to move back toward the level where the gap occurred. As its name suggests, you will see this type of gap more often than the others on this list.

- Breakaway Gap: Breakaway gaps occur during periods of high volatility or significant news, often signaling the beginning of a new trend. Breakaway gaps are less likely to get filled quickly. They often mark a significant change in market sentiment, leading the price to continue moving in the direction of the gap. A breakaway gap can give you price action that moves in one direction all day long, rather than the up

& down waves that we see so often with 'normal' days.

- Exhaustion Gap: Exhaustion gaps form at the end of a strong trend and signal a potential reversal in the price direction. These gaps are more likely to get filled as traders reassess the prevailing trend and look for opportunities to take profits or reverse their positions.

- Continuation Gap: Continuation gaps occur within an ongoing trend and indicate a temporary pause or consolidation before the trend continues. These gaps can go either way, getting filled or leading to further continuation of the trend. The outcome depends on the strength of the underlying trend and market sentiment.

Common and breakaway gaps are the easiest to spot, and you'll see those two more often than exhaustion or continuation gaps. It's important to note that while gaps often have some predictability in their movement, there's no guarantee a gap will do what you think it will do. As I've said before and will say again, **the market will do what it wants, when it wants.**

Speaking of predictability: gaps are one of the main reasons I do not like to hold a position overnight. The fact is, gaps introduce unpredictability and they happen often—so I like avoiding them at all costs. And the only way to be 100%

certain of avoiding a gap is by NOT holding a position overnight.

So back to my premarket prep: I can easily do steps 1-9 within 30 minutes, because it usually only takes me about 10-15 minutes to study the pre-market & daily chart price action. Now is probably a good time to explain what I mean by 'price action' since it's the most basic building block of trading... price action is to trading what DNA is to crime scene analysis—without price action, there is no trading.

PRICE ACTION

Inevitably, one of the first things beginning traders ask is, *"What is price action?"* They've all heard the term bandied about everywhere, but might not know what it means. In the simplest terms, price action is the literal movement of the price as the trading day progresses, which can go three ways—up *(bullish movement)*, down *(bearish movement)*, or sideways *(consolidation)*. If the price of the underlying stock I'm trading is consolidating I would probably say, *"This price action is garbage"* because with my strategy, I actually make money as price rises or falls—but not while it's moving sideways.

You could just as easily interchange the term 'price action' for 'price changes' or 'price movement'... but price *action* definitely sounds cooler.

Here are a few terms and concepts related to price action in day trading. They might not all make perfect sense to you right now, but they will after I take you through a trade step by step.

- Visual Analysis: This simply means observing and analyzing the price movement directly on a chart, using candlesticks. I rely on more than *just* price action when I'm deciding what & how to trade each day, but price action analysis ALWAYS has more to do with the decisions I make than any other piece of information.

- Candlestick Patterns: As stated above, price action analysis always involves candlesticks and the study of candlestick *patterns*. These patterns form as a result of price movement and provide visual clues about potential trend changes, reversals, or continuation. A pattern is simply two or more candlesticks side by side on a chart. For the sake of not asking you to read an extra 100 pages, I'm going to omit detailed explanation of every type of pattern than can occur on a chart. We WILL talk about the most relevant & important ones, just not *all* of them. There are plenty of good books and online videos that explain every pattern in existence in great detail. If you really want to take a deep-dive into candlestick patterns I suggest finishing this book first and *then* doing that. I am going to teach you all of the essential patterns you need to know in this book.

- Support and Resistance: Identifying support and resistance levels through price action analysis helps traders understand where the price might reverse, consolidate, or continue its movement. Identifying valid support & resistance levels in combination with identifying valid candlestick patterns is the best way to have confidence in your trade ideas. More on this in a minute.

- Trend lines: Drawing trend lines on a chart helps identify the direction and continuation of a trend. We can use price action to determine where our trend lines go, thus helping us identify support and resistance levels. Drawing trend lines is a really effective way to not only predict the direction price will go, but also identify when a legitimate change in direction is occurring. Take a look at this example:

Now I'm going to explain how I might trade based on price action and trend lines.

On this 1 minute AAPL chart we see the 200 EMA, the Keltner Channels, and our trend line. We see that price was rising at the left hand side of this image, and then about 15 minutes in, a potential reversal appears, and price action gets choppy for the next 10 minutes. Once that huge red bar appears 26 minutes in, price falls to the lower line on the Keltner Channels and settles there. At this point, I would be comfortable getting in short. I wouldn't necessarily feel *confident* here, since price is still technically above the 200 EMA *(that horizontal white line cutting across the image)* But it's just *barely* above it at this point, so I would feel OK getting in short here.

As price makes its way lower and lower, you can see that it always bounces off the thick white trend line that we have drawn based on the lower highs created at the 15, 19, 26, and

37 minute candles. I like to see at least 3 higher highs or lower lows before I feel confident that a legitimate trend is actually developing.

'Higher highs' and 'lower lows' are always present whenever a trend is developing in either direction, since price almost never goes in a straight line up or down. There's usually a 'stepping' effect as the trend works. For example, in bearish moves we'll see a lot of red candles and then a few green ones as price attempts to come back up, and then more red candles will follow if the bearish trend is actually strong *(and vice-versa for bullish moves).*

Continuing with the above example, if we follow price action we can see it continue to trend down all the way until the bottom wick of the red candle that touches our 176.29 marker. If I were in short on this trade, I would have been closing out contracts slowly as the price fell. At each one of the big red candles I'd be selling a few contracts with each wash, locking in profits as I took the ride down.

When I saw the three green candles to the immediate right of our red candle at 176.29, my Spidey-Senses would tingle and I'd start thinking about closing whatever contracts I still had left. I wouldn't have done anything drastic at this point, because it's still possible this is just a quick flag before price continues lower.

But once we reached the highlighted oval section where the trend break occurred, I'd definitely close out some *(if not all)* of my remaining contracts, because a trend break is significant. What is the 'trend break?' We can see on the left of the image, each time the candles bump up against the thick white line *(the trend line)* the bulls aren't strong enough to send it through. In this case, that trend line acts as a resistance level *(it would be called a support level if the trend was going up instead of down)*.

So when price *does* finally break through an established trend line, that more often than not signals a reversal about to happen, as it does in this case. So if I did have any remaining contracts, I would definitely have closed them out on that huge green candle that sends price from the center to the top line on the Keltner Channels. Even if I closed out my last few contracts for a loss here that's OK, because the *overall* trade as a whole would still be profitable, since I would have been locking in profits during the ride down from the highs.

Step 7: Place alerts at key levels of support & resistance

Let's continue with more detail on support and resistance levels, and why they're so important. In addition to interpreting price action, doing technical analysis to identify valid support and resistance levels is one of the most important factors in successful trading. Literally everything that happens during a trading day is connected to support and resistance levels. These levels determine the probable *(but never definite)* places where price action might get hung up. It's very important to identify these levels correctly because no matter what's happening with price at the moment, a valid support or resistance level will give you clues about what could happen *next*, based on how price reacts to those levels.

Here's an explanation of support and resistance levels in day trading:

- Support Level: A support level is a price level at which a security's price tends to stop falling and may even bounce back upward. It represents a level where buying interest outweighs selling pressure. Support levels are often good buying opportunities. When the price reaches a support level, watch for both continuation or reversal. If the price bounces off of the support level and reverses, that could be a good time to go long. If it slices through the level with conviction, that can be a good time to enter *(or add to)* a short position.

- Resistance Level: A resistance level is a price level at which a security's price tends to stop rising and may encounter selling pressure. It represents a level where selling interest outweighs buying pressure. The same opportunities I just mentioned above are at play here, but reversed.

- Role Reversal: Once a support level is breached, it often becomes a new resistance level. Similarly, when a resistance level is broken, it can turn into a new support level. This phenomenon is known as 'role reversal.'

- Importance of Volume: Volume often plays a crucial role in confirming the significance of support and resistance levels. Higher volume at a support or resistance level can validate the level's importance and indicate stronger buying or selling interest.

- Psychological Factors: Psychological factors can influence support and resistance levels. Round numbers (*e.g.*, $100, $50) and previous highs or lows can act as psychological support and resistance points due to the attention they attract from traders.

- Trend lines: These can be used to identify support and resistance levels. An upward trend line acts as support, while a downward trend line serves as resistance.

- Moving Averages: Moving averages, especially longer-term ones like the 200-day EMA, can act as dynamic support or resistance levels. Prices often react around these averages.

- Breakouts and Pullbacks: Breakouts occur when the price moves above a resistance level or below a support level. These breakouts can lead to significant price movements. After a breakout, I will frequently look for a pullback to the broken resistance *(now support)* level to enter in the direction of the breakout.

One important thing to remember about identifying daily support and resistance levels: **THE MOST RECENT LEVELS ARE ALWAYS MORE RELEVANT THAN OLDER LEVELS.** Look at the image below for an example of what I'm talking about.

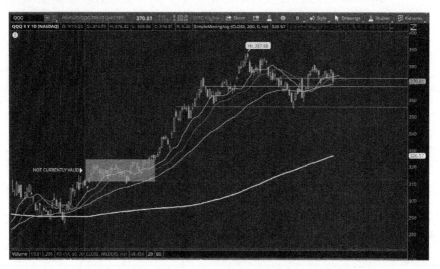

We see the daily price action for QQQ. Notice the two horizontal lines that are fairly close together towards the top of the chart, both close to the current day's price.

These 2 levels are each *valid* levels, for 2 reasons:

1. Price has touched each one of these levels multiple times

2. Those multiple touches all occur fairly recently

What this means is—both of these levels can act as strong support or resistance levels during intraday trading. And depending on how price reacts to these levels, we can predict where it could go from there.

For example: at the moment this screenshot was taken, the price of QQQ is sitting squarely in the middle of these 2 upper levels. If the market opens tomorrow and price rips through the upper line, I would then consider that upper level to be a *support* level, since it's shown to be a level that price has gotten 'hung up' on multiple times recently.

If the opposite happened and price sliced below the bottom of these 2 levels, then that level would then act as a *resistance* level, and the next level I'd pay attention to as a *support* level would be the area around the lowest of our three horizontal levels.

Notice the highlighted box at the bottom left of the image that says 'NOT CURRENTLY VALID'. This area is much too far away from our current price to actually *mean anything* right now. A novice trader might say, *"Look at how much activity there is right here, this has to be a valid level."*

Two problems with that thought. First, that level is about 50 POINTS BELOW where we're currently sitting. That's a MASSIVE difference in price, and doesn't even belong in the conversation of current price action. Maybe price will get back down there *months* from now, but certainly not any time in the next few days or week.

Secondly, that confluence of price action in the highlighted box happened *months earlier,* which makes it practically meaningless to us right now. The further back we go from *today,* the less importance a level should have. The very top level has the most significance, because where price has been getting hung up most *recently.*

Recency bias should always be a factor when you're determining your daily support & resistance levels. That highlighted area might make sense if you were swing trading and thinking months or a year in advance, but is has nothing to do with our day trading levels.

And now here's a real world example of how these levels can affect you while trading:

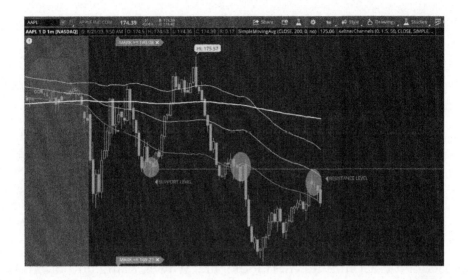

Above we see a 1-minute chart on AAPL. Pay attention to the horizontal price level line in the middle of the image. This is an intraday support & resistance level, meaning—it wasn't created due to trends or price action from last week or last month—this level established itself today while trading was happening. Notice three oval highlighted sections here.

For the first two oval highlights starting from the left, this horizontal line represents a SUPPORT level, meaning price action is being *supported* at that level... it doesn't want to drop below this point. We can see there's a 10-minute stretch about an hour into the trading day where price just holds at this level. This is a crucial time for the stock, because it's either going to bounce and take off higher to the upside, or it's going to show weakness and break below that line.

You can see that the price *does* break below this line, and now that same horizontal line which was a support level is now a resistance level. You can see that about 20 minutes after that, price tried to break through the level to the upside but failed. The level that was a support level at the very beginning of the day is a resistance level about 1 hour into the trading day.

This happens all the time. It's VERY rare that a stock's movement will *only* rise or fall all day long without any significant pullbacks in either direction. Most days, the price action on a 1 minute chart looks like waves, rising and falling throughout the day. And that's fine! You can make plenty of money just 'riding the waves' of price action throughout the day. If you become skilled at knowing when to jump in, and when to get out, that's half the battle. Timing is everything.

When you strip away ALL of the extra stuff and get to the heart of what trading actually IS, this is all we do—open trades, and close trades. Get into positions, then get out of them. If you can develop your ability to read the charts correctly and learn how to *enter and exit at the right time*, you WILL be successful.

And here's where the skill lies. Nobody is born with a 'natural sense of timing' for trading, the way some people can just sit down at a drum set and play a perfect beat without ever having a drum lesson... No, this is *all* learned. Figuring out how it all comes together is 100% a learned skill.

How do the candlesticks interact to create patterns, and how do those patterns combine with the indicators to give you the clues you'll need to uncover, in order to determine where price is going next? Trading is like a mystery that unfolds every day. The charts are giving you the clues, but ultimately you'll need to solve the mystery yourself.

This is what I aim to teach you in this book. I know there's a LOT of information here, and it might not all make sense right away, but if you stick with it and put it into practice, it will all get easier and easier as the days pass.

TIME FRAMES

A person can trade on any time frame they'd like. You can choose literally any minute denomination and set your chart to that time frame. For example, you *could* decide to trade with an 18 minute chart *(I don't know what anyone would want to do that, but you could)*. The time frame set to your chart is an average of the high & low prices from that period—so a 1 minute candle is the average of high & low price of the past minute. The 15 minute chart is the average of the highs & lows of the last 15 minutes, and so on.

These are the time frames I use when day trading, and why I use them.

1 MINUTE:

This is the ONLY time frame I look at when entering *and* exiting positions because it is the shortest clock-based time interval you can use, therefore it gives you the most immediate representation of price right NOW. If you've already made a profit on a trade and you're ready to close your position, the 1 minute chart lets you choose the EXACT minute to exit that position. Likewise, if you've been eyeing price action looking for an entry and you've identified buy signals, you can get in at the exact minute you choose to enter based on the immediate price action of the 1 minute candles.

Although you could have your chart set to whatever time frame you'd like, and enter or exit at will...it's not very helpful looking at a daily chart that might barely move over the course of hours when attempting to find the perfect moment to get in or out. For example, if you're looking at the daily chart of AMD while trying to decide when to enter during the morning session—that daily chart may look exactly the same at 9:00 as it will at 9:15. But if you had been looking at the 1 minute chart, you could have seen the price rising and falling 15 times in that same span of time. So obviously, it's in your best interest to see the immediate price action throughout the day, wherever you are in the process of opening or closing the trade.

15 MINUTE:

The 15 minute chart is a good 'in-between' chart to study when you're trying to uncover the beginnings of a trend or the end of a strong move in either direction. It's a short enough time frame to give you a decent connection to recent price action, but still long enough to spot when a trend is just beginning or ending.

I will usually view the 15 minute chart using the normal Japanese candlesticks *(like the 1 minute chart)* but sometimes I'll also check the Heiken Ashi charts with the 15 minute interval, just to get another perspective.

30 MINUTE:

The 30 minute chart is good for identifying intraday trends that last approximately 30 minutes to 1 hour. This is very useful for seeing the continued strength of a trend that's already formed, and seeing when a shorter-term trend might be losing strength. This is also a good chart to view when trying to spot a reversal.

1 HOUR:

The 1 hour chart is good for identifying even longer term trends, such as trends that might last for a majority of the day. I like to look at this chart for reversals, because the 1 hour chart is much less prone to 'fake outs' than the 1 or 15 minute charts are.

The size of the candles on the 1 hour chart can be telling, because even if we're looking at consecutive candles of the same color—if one is long and the next one is significantly shorter and the third one is a doji, this signals slowing momentum and a possible reversal for the longer term. I don't normally keep a 1 hour chart on my screens full time, but I do check it often throughout my daily trading session.

Remember this: when you're looking at longer time frames,, you have more stability in the overall direction of a trend—but also less accurate visual feedback of price action relating to the current moment. **For the NOW, always look at the 1 minute chart. For the longer-term 'big picture', look at longer time frames.** And then connect the dots to see how current price action fits in with a longer term trend.

DAILY:

The daily chart is the most important chart in determining valid support & resistance levels, which are the levels that help us decide where to go long or short. It's also very helpful in identifying where a longer-term trend may reverse. For example, if we've seen a steady uptrend in daily levels for 3 or 4 consecutive days but then get a bearish engulfing candle, this could be a sign that the bullish trend is over and we're about to reverse soon.

The daily chart is also extremely useful in combination with premarket data. I can't believe how many traders don't pay any attention to premarket data simply because there's less volume and therefore more volatility. Combining premarket data with the daily chart can be very helpful in predicting the overall tone of the trading day.

For example, if I see waning bullish pressure on the daily chart, and the previous day's candle was a doji… and then we get a gap down before the market opens, I'm going to lean short at the open. Of course, there's always the possibility that the stock will rip right at the open, but that's because—say it with me… **the market will do what it wants, whenever it wants.**

It's easy to see how someone might get discouraged and say, *"Well if the market will do whatever it wants, whenever it wants, then what's the point? Isn't this whole process futile?"* If you think like this, then you're missing the whole point. If you want to be a worker bee, go get a job and take orders from a boss. Once I decided I wasn't going to do that shit anymore, I became a wolf. And here we are.

Like I've said already—my strategy gives me a 70-80% daily win rate. Am I *not* going to trade because I have a 30% chance of losing? Hell no. Buy the ticket, take the ride. Get comfortable with the fact that you *will* have losing trades, and losing days. And those days will hurt. But understand that you will ALSO go on ridiculous winning streaks that will make you say to yourself, *"Is it really this easy?"* And the elation you'll feel on those days will far outweigh the pain you'll feel on your losing days.

Just like with indicators, there is no 'magic timeframe' that will always give you winning trades. The secret is YOU using your mind and your trading skill to put the pieces together and make the best decisions based on the information currently available to you. The totality of day trading is a bit like putting together a jigsaw puzzle. You can see each individual piece on the table, but you need to imagine what the finished puzzle will look like in your mind before you consider all of the different possibilities that exist from the different combinations of pieces. It's one of the many things I love about day trading—using nothing but the power of my own mind *(and sometimes a bit of luck)* to be successful.

YOU HAVE TOMORROW, AND THE DAY AFTER THAT

There are approximately 250 trading days per year. And that means you don't have to trade every single day to make a living doing this. I know you *want* to trade every day so you can see that immediate income fattening up your trading account on a daily basis *(after all, if you go full- time this is the money you'll need to pay your bills).* Trust me, I want to see daily profits as well.

But the fact is: some days, things just *don't* set up very well. Certain days I'll see a pre-market setup that looks PERFECT just a few minutes before the open—and when that happens, I'll hit the trade with BIG size. There's nothing like the feeling I get when the daily chart tells me it should be a green day in pre-market, and then I see the right side of a mature double-bottom forming 2 minutes before the open. Those are the days when I go big right from the start, because my technical analysis and my interpretation of the chart patterns tells me I can feel confident doing so.

If the pre-market price action is looking flat, a lot of times I'll just sit back and wait until the candlesticks actually form a real trend before getting involved. What do I mean by a 'real trend?' It means a trend that's NOT a fake out... I don't interpret two or three 1-minute candles going in the same direction as a mature trend. I WAIT until the candlesticks and the Alligator and the EMA's are creating an easily identifiable up or down trend, and then I'll wait until I spot a pullback, then get in right before the bounce. And of course, I'm looking at the 1 minute chart as I do this.

So to summarize- every morning BEFORE the market opens, you'll need to check the daily chart and the premarket trading data, and connect the dots. What do you see? Do you notice any particular candlestick patterns jumping out at you? It's always important to get a plan formulated in your mind before the market opens: "If it does *this*, I'm doing *this*." But remember, even though you always want to have a plan—we can only make decisions based on the information available to us at the time—so if a situation suddenly changes, you'll need to be able to adapt to that changing situation.

There have been many days where premarket data & daily chart analysis has made it look like price action would go one way, but then as soon as the market opened it went the other way. This is OK- just adapt and ride the wave. You can win whether the market goes up or down. All you need to do is become skilled at knowing when to get in, and when to get out. Timing is everything.

CHAPTER 6

The Proper Mindset

"Excellence is never an accident. It is always the result of high intention, sincere effort, and intelligent execution; it represents the wise choice of many alternatives - choice, not chance, determines your destiny." — Aristotle

Before you even begin thinking about actually trading with real money, it's important to get yourself in the correct mindset to be able to handle all of the emotions you're about to experience.

Day trading stock options is one of the most self-reflective and personally illuminating experiences you will ever have. There is no way to understate how much you will learn about yourself through this process. You will discover *who you are* at your core, as it relates to so many aspects of your own psychology: how you handle pressure, how you manage risk, your ability to strategize, your ability to stay disciplined, your ability to resist the emotions of greed and fear, your reaction to huge wins and losses... and the list goes on and on. I would even argue that day trading can give you a level of self-discovery that rivals seeing a therapist.

I'm sure a lot of you are already familiar with the concept of 'paper trading' and think that's where we'll start—but there's one stop we need to make first. before you even start paper trading, I want you to take at least a month to simply WATCH the charts of the tickers you're interested in trading. That's right—do nothing but *watch* for at least an entire month.

I know that's not what you want to hear at the beginning of your journey. You want to dive in head first and make ALL the money right NOW. But remember the old saying, *"Learn to walk before you run."* Yeah, it's corny... but it's also TRUE. You will only hurt yourself if you start placing trades before you've truly familiarized yourself with all of the information and discoveries and *"Oh shit!"* moments you'll inevitably have as you begin your journey. It's MUCH better to experience those 'oh shit' moments while you're simply *looking* at the charts, rather than also losing hundreds or thousands of dollars at the same time.

There is no specific waiting period you need to abide by, but you *should* wait until the charts don't surprise you as frequently. Even I still get surprised occasionally by a move that the market makes, but for the most part, when I look at the day-to-day price action I think to myself, *"I've seen that before."* You want to get to that place in your mind of not being surprised often. Once you're there, then it's a lot easier to have confidence in every trade you take.

A lot of stock market players make trades that are closer to gambling than trading with any type of fundamental strategy. If you're thinking of going all-in on the next meme stock, why not just go to Vegas and put it all on the Roulette wheel instead? At least you'd get a fun trip out of it instead of watching your money evaporate on a screen.

I'm not saying these plays *never* work... because every play in the market works for *somebody*. What I'm saying is, your chances of success with trades like these are minuscule compared to trading a legit, solid strategy like the one I've developed. Would you rather make $6,000 profit on 3% of your trades while losing the other 97% of the time, or make $600 on 70% of your trades while only losing 30% of the time?

If you want longevity, strive for consistency OVER home-runs. You've heard the phrase 'slow and steady wins the race,' right? This is basically '*small* and steady wins the race.' Smaller profits *(at first),* with steady consistency. Over time you can scale up once you build your trading account, and *then* you'll start making big money. But at first, just focus on achieving consistency.

If you only chase the money, you'll find yourself taking unnecessary risks, potentially losing more often than you win. But if you chase consistency, the money will come consistently—and when you DO lose *(it WILL happen),* you'll lose less than what you win in your green trades.

Get this phrase burned into your mind: **The stock market can do anything it wants, at any time.** Don't ever forget it, because this is an absolute truth. And that's why, NO MATTER how perfect your technical analysis, or your preparation, or your ability to read price action is—you will ALWAYS experience losses at some point, even when everything looks like you 'should' be right.

We can only react to what we see before us on the charts, and once you become a skilled trader, more often than not you'll be correct. But sometimes the market just does what it wants, regardless of what you thought it would do based on your analysis.

SIGN OF THE TIMES

Some people day trade simply because they want to see fresh money in their account every day. I use shorter time frames because shorter time frames give me more confidence in my ability to predict price action—and in trading, the more predictability we have, the better chance of success we have.

Here's a good analogy about how different time frames can affect your trades: If I asked you, *"How confident are you in predicting how you'll feel 5 minutes from now?"* Chances are, you're about 99% confident that you know exactly how you'll feel 5 minutes from now. But if I asked, *"How confident are you in predicting how you'll feel tomorrow?"* And what about next week? Next month?

The further away we move from right NOW, the less confident we can be about everything in life. A giant asteroid is not going to destroy the world in the next 10 minutes. But sometime within the next 10 months? Who knows?

This is a key element of why I trade the way I do. There are plenty of traders who make a great living swing trading *(which involves the position staying open for many days or even weeks)*, but I personally like being able to look at a chart and feel confident based on what I see *now* that I know where the price is going, at least within the next 15 to 60 minutes. That's why day trading is so powerful.

Always analyze your charts with your perceived time frame in mind. What this means is: If you're a long-term investor, you probably don't care about what the market's going to do in the next hour, because you're in it for the long haul. The next hour represents a fraction of the total amount of time you plan on being involved. You want to know what the market's going to do in a few months or a year from now.

For ME, an hour represents roughly 100% of the amount of time I'm planning on being involved in the trade. I'm not concerned with where the market's going to be next month. Whether it's up or down next month makes no difference to me.

I care about what the market is going to do today, and more importantly what it's doing *right now*, therefore I focus all of my attention on the 1 minute, 15 minute and 30 minute chart *(and I check the daily chart during premarket)*. Here's a concept that will save you a lot of money and headaches: **only focus on what you need to focus on, and tune out the rest of the noise.**

A little analogy to expand on this concept: I'm a lifelong musician, and back in my 20's I recorded and toured for many years with a punk rock band. Of course we made no money, but making money is NOT why you decide to start a punk rock band. Anyways, the point of the story is—we'd be on tour, and of course we'd already have our tour schedule, so we knew where we were going to play the next day, and the day after that, and so on.

When I knew we'd be playing at CBGB's in New York next week, but *that* night we were playing in Amarillo, Texas... obviously I was more excited to go to NYC and play at CBGB's, but my focus each day *(no matter where we were)* was on *that night's performance.* I was thinking about *that* club, in *that* city, for *that* crowd on *that* particular day.

The same thing holds true for all aspects of trading. Don't even worry about where you think the stock will be next week, or get excited thinking about how much money you'll be making next year... focus on everything you can do RIGHT NOW, to make your trading as profitable as possible TODAY. Tomorrow will come, and when tomorrow does come you should be in the moment then, just as you should be in *this* moment right *now.*

I think about trading as if I'm delivering a pizza *(30 minutes or less!)* So on a perfect day I'm in and out of all my trades within 30 minutes to an hour maximum. Of course, things don't play out this perfectly every day. Sometimes I'll need to work it a bit longer, because the thing I *thought* would develop very quickly actually took a lot longer to develop. Sometimes I'll need to work the trade all day long. That happens. You can still be right, but you won't always be right within your ideal time frame.

Some days I'll be in the process of peeling out contracts and locking in profits as the trade is going in my favor. As I'm doing this, maybe I'll still have ONE more contract open and suddenly the price drops out like crazy, losing 10% or more on 1 candle. Depending on a lot of factors, I may decide to keep that position open, or even ADD to it knowing that it would lower my average price if the trade comes back in my direction. There will be a lot more discussion about this in the 'managing the trade' chapter.

How much risk I choose to accept is always situational. If I'm holding ONE lower priced contract (*like something around $100*) and this happens, I'm more likely to keep it open, take the ride and see what happens. After all, the MOST I could lose would be the price of that one contract. But if that one contract cost me $400, I'll be a lot quicker to close it out when it starts going against me, to minimize losses. Everything is situational. What works in one scenario might not work in a different one.

DESIRE AND FEAR

There are only 2 basic motivations in human existence: desire and fear. Every action that anyone has ever made, since the beginning of time, has been the response to one of those two motivations.

Either we *want* something to happen to us, or we're *afraid* of something happening to us. These same 2 motivations lie at the heart of trading. Every move we make, we make it because either we desire a certain thing, or we're afraid of a certain thing. BOTH of these motivations are valid and necessary to navigate life successfully.

If a person lived their entire life motivated *only* by desire, they would probably live fairly dangerously and might not live very long. On the other hand, a person who lived their life motivated *only* by fear would probably not have very many exciting stories to tell, and would almost certainly not be very fun at parties.

Although I'm naturally more of a *desire* than *fear* type of person, there are plenty of situations in life when being motivated by fear is completely understandable. For example, you probably have insurance on your car. This is an example of a very logical fear-based motivation. When you purchase insurance, you're not thinking, *"I can't wait to get into an accident so I can file a claim using my brand new insurance policy!"* You're thinking, *"I'm happy I won't be personally liable for an accident now that I have insurance."*

Here's an opportunity to stop and reflect, and maybe gain some introspective wisdom. Ask yourself this question: *Why exactly do you want to day trade for a living?* Is it because you just want to make tons of money and live the flashy, finance bro life? Is it because you'd like to have a bit of 'income insurance' to supplement your salary from your day job? Is it because you're afraid you might *lose* your job soon and want to develop a self-taught skill that can make you money?

Although each of these different answers could have led you to the reality that you're here now reading this book, the motivation behind each one is different. The more you know yourself and understand *why* you do the things you do, the better equipped you'll be *(psychologically speaking)* to handle the ups and downs that will happen as you do this.

OPTIMISM ISN'T A CHOICE, IT'S A NECESSITY

This next bit of psychology is extremely important. You should ALWAYS have the mindset of, *"I'm going to WIN with this trade."* But at the same time, you need to always be prepared to accept a loss when that loss inevitably happens. Those two concepts are not mutually exclusive. This is similar to the psychology of any great athlete, who always enters the game with a positive mindset, yet knows they will need to accept losses at some point.

I think about having an optimistic outlook the way I think about breathing. It's not something I've decided to do. It's something I HAVE to do. If you don't already have a positive, growth mindset *before* you take on this challenge, you've lost before you even begin. You MUST have an optimistic outlook if you want to be a successful day trader.

Remember this: **It's OK to lose in a trade. It's never OK to think you're about to lose** *before* **you enter the trade.** If you notice your inner voice telling you, *"This will never work"* before placing a trade, <u>DO NOT PLACE THE TRADE.</u> Step away from the computer. Work on your mindset for as long as you need to before risking real money. Simply watch the charts until you start to gain confidence in what you see. Study the movement of the candlesticks and use the knowledge contained in this book to predict the direction of price action. The more times you get it right, the stronger your confidence grows.

Next, move on to paper trading, using the same size you'll be using when it's real money. See how that goes. If you're doing well, trade after trade will come out green, and your confidence will build further. When you're finally ready, it's time to place a REAL trade. And now, that same inner voice that was saying, *"This will never work"* will be telling you, *"I know what I'm doing. This is going to work."*

FOCUS ON THE CHART, NOT ON THE NEWS

When I'm trading I don't place much importance on CNBC or any other financial news. One of the reasons for this is because I trade the same handful of stocks every day, so I don't need to know a lot of the minutiae regarding specific stocks & company profiles. I focus on THE CHART. The candlesticks, the patterns those candlesticks make, my support & resistance lines, and the very specific set of indicators on my charts. That's it.

When you focus on the news, you trade the 'what ifs' that the news inevitably gives you. For example, if AMD is set to release a new chip next week, and you see a news report saying exactly that: *"AMD will be releasing a new chip next week!"* You've already established an unconscious long bias for AMD simply because of that news. You'll think to yourself: NEW CHIP = STOCK PRICE WILL RISE = BUY AMD CALLS!

But what if the new AMD chip is actually crap? What if the street decides the new chip is far inferior to NVDA's latest chip? There are SO many things that can go in any direction when you use news *(especially speculative news)* to influence your trading.

Anything theoretical that isn't right in front of your face is just that: theoretical. It's speculation. It *could* happen, or it could *not* happen. But the candlesticks represent what *is* happening RIGHT NOW, and the more immediate you are in your trading, the more edge you have. If you can really identify the reality of what's happening *right now*, then you'll have the best chance of predicting the move in the very near future. So, to wrap up this chapter on mindset—focus on these things BEFORE you place your first trade:

- Ask yourself what your true motivations are for wanting to trade

- Stay focused on the correct *(short term)* time frames— stay in the NOW

- Trade the chart, not the news. Tune out all the noise that comes from speculation

- ALWAYS approach every trade with an optimistic prediction of the outcome

CHAPTER 7

What to Trade?

"If you don't live it, it won't come out of your horn."
—Charlie Parker

Before you get started trading real options with real money, obviously you'll need to decide *what* to trade, *how* to trade, and how to measure your *success* with that trade. Before I get into the details of exactly what and how I personally trade, I'll give you a quick overview of a few of the most popular trading strategies, then I'll get into *my* strategy and compare/contrast it to some other popular strategies.

SOME POPULAR TRADING STRATEGIES

- Trend Trading: This strategy involves identifying and trading in the direction of the prevailing trend. Trend traders look for stocks or options that are consistently moving up or down, and aim to enter positions in the direction of the trend. Technical analysis tools like moving averages and trend lines are often used to identify trends. This is a *huge* part of my strategy.

- Momentum Trading: Momentum traders look for stocks or options with significant price movements and high trading volumes. They aim to ride the momentum generated by these price surges and exit the position before the trend loses steam. This is similar to trend trading.

- Pattern Trading: Pattern traders focus on chart patterns, such as head and shoulders, double tops/bottoms, triangles, and flags. They look for these recognizable patterns to identify potential entry and exit points based on historical price behavior.

- Range Trading: Range traders focus on stocks or options that are trading within a specific price range. They buy near the support level and sell near the resistance level, anticipating that the price will bounce back and forth within the range. Technical indicators like the Relative Strength Index (RSI) and support/resistance levels help identify potential entry and exit points.

- Breakout Trading: Breakout traders look for stocks or options that are experiencing a significant price movement beyond a well-defined support or resistance level. They enter the trade when the price breaks out of the range, anticipating a continuation of the price movement in the breakout direction.

- Scalping: Scalpers make numerous quick trades throughout the day, aiming to profit from small price movements. They hold positions for only a few minutes and execute multiple trades to accumulate small gains that can add up over the course of the day.

- Contrarian Trading: Contrarian traders take positions against the prevailing market sentiment. When the market is overly bullish, they may look for short-selling opportunities, and when the market is overly bearish, they may seek to buy. This strategy relies on the belief that market sentiment can lead to overreactions and create opportunities for profits.

- News-Based Trading: Traders using this strategy focus on trading opportunities resulting from significant news events, such as earnings reports, economic data releases, or company announcements. They quickly react to the news and attempt to profit from the resulting price movements.

- Pivot Point Trading: Pivot points are levels calculated based on the previous day's high, low, and closing prices. Day traders use pivot points to identify potential support and resistance levels. They take trades based on how the price behaves around these pivot levels.

THE LONE WOLF SECRET SAUCE

I can't say my strategy is 100% unique. At this point in history, *nobody* can say that... it's kind of like any band claiming that they wrote a *'completely original* pop song'. All of the possible chord combinations have already been combined. But you can still combine things that have already been combined while adding your own 'secret sauce' to it... and that's what I'm doing.

From the above list of the most popular types of trading strategies, my unique style combines TREND, MOMENTUM and PATTERN tactics. I don't do contrarian trading and I don't often pay attention to financial news while I'm trading. I will sometimes scalp *(rarely)* and I will check the pivot points if I'm just looking for additional levels that could act as support or resistance, but since I always trade with the trend, I'll use pivot points as an additional way of determining the right time to *exit* a position rather than entering one.

Why am I confident in my strategy? Well, from my own experience trading it day after day:

- It doesn't rely on outside sources for entries *(news cycles, pundits, 'financial influencers')*

- It's so simple, even an absolute beginner can wrap their head around it

- When done correctly, it gives consistent returns of at least 10% daily

- It works in short time frames, short enough so that you can trade in the first hour and then enjoy   your day.

Just like learning the ins & outs of the market itself, doing research into the gazillion different tickers listed can be overwhelming. But fear not, young wolf, I have great news! Remember back at the beginning of this book when I said, *"Although there are a million things you could learn about… you don't need to learn everything about everything."* EXACTLY the same thing applies to choosing which stocks to trade. You can make a healthy living trading no more than a handful of different tickers. That's what I've been doing for years.

There's no reason for a person to spend endless amounts of time researching the fundamentals of a bunch of small companies very few people have ever heard of, or scouring the feeds for news about said companies. Of course, you *can* do that if you want to… but that's not something I've ever been interested in. I'm the kind of guy who doesn't need to know how to rebuild the engine—as long as the car gets me there, I'm happy.

Some people love to nerd out with research and graphs and charts… if that's you, then cool—more power to you. But if you're like me and you'd rather spend your free time doing something like riding your motorcycle or playing guitar or traveling to distant, exotic lands, you're in luck. A small number of blue chip tickers is ALL you need to be very successful. The only 'research' you'll need to do is the regular morning review of the price action on the daily chart and the pre-market movement... but that's something you'd need to do that no matter what you decided to trade.

In my entire trading career I've traded *maybe* 15 different tickers in total. My MAIN plays have always been SPY *(an ETF that tracks the S&P 500 index)*, QQQ *(an ETF that tracks the Nasdaq index)*, AAPL, META and AMD. Occasionally I'll trade NVDA, INTEL, or some other random ticker *(usually a tech stock)* that catches my fancy, but that's rare. I would say at least 50% of my profits have come from trading SPY, AMD and META. In fact, some people ONLY trade SPY and nothing else. So if you're looking for a good place to start, I recommend using the SPY as your guinea pig before moving on to anything else.

Why do I prefer the tickers I just listed? Two reasons: liquidity and predictability. Liquidity works like this: when you have a TON of volume on a certain ticker, that means there's a lot of people all wanting to trade that same ticker, so it's very easy to get 'in and out' of the trade. A stock with HIGH liquidity is like a Honda Civic. You can find one anywhere, they're easy to buy and easy to sell. A stock with

LOW liquidity is like a Rolls-Royce Phantom. A LOT harder to find, and a lot more complicated to buy AND sell.

Every ticker I trade has very high liquidity, meaning—I'll never have a problem getting into or out of my position. The second I click the 'buy' button I'm in the position, and the second I click the 'sell' button I'm out. In addition to the stocks I trade having high liquidity, one other reason I can get in or out so quickly is because I only use MARKET ORDERS.

A market order essentially means, *"Get me in or out as fast as possible at whatever price you give me."* Now this sounds scary at first... you might be thinking, *"The listed price is $250 per contract, but what if I get filled at $280 per contract?"* That's a logical fear to have, but when you trade high-volume, large-cap stocks, you WILL have plenty of liquidity. What this means is: the bid/ask spread *(the difference between the listed price and the price you pay)* will be very small. The larger the cap *(and the more volume traded)* the smaller the spread.

Anyone who's seen "The Wolf of Wall Street" has probably dreamed of getting filthy rich trading penny stocks like Jordan Belfort. This is not what I do. That's a much riskier way to trade *(in fact over 90% of penny stocks fail)*. My strategy relies on predictability. I'd rather have an 80% chance of making 10% every day than have a 10% chance of making 80% on the day. This also takes us into the area of RISK

MANAGEMENT, which we will break down later on. For now, let's continue to focus on why I trade what I trade.

On to the second reason, which is: predictability. You might be thinking, *"HOW can you even use a word like 'predictability'… this is the STOCK MARKET!"* And you would be correct. The market is inherently dangerous, even when you DO know what you're doing. There are never guarantees in trading, and we know this. But when you know what you're doing, you can be right approximately 70-80% of the time. And that's more than enough 'being right' to make a healthy living.

So in *absolute* terms, NO, the market is NOT predictable. The market will do whatever it wants, whenever it wants. What I mean is: by using my strategy and only trading large-cap, blue chip stocks *(or ETF's like SPY)*… when you look at the charts, study the price action and realize what you're looking at—you will see a certain amount of structured, predictable movement.

Don't believe me? Then do this right now: pull up SPY on your trading platform and set your time frame to the daily chart. Observe the motion of the price action. It looks like waves, doesn't it? Rising, falling, up and down… patterns of repetition. Of course it's not exact, but it does have some cohesion as you look at the days or weeks of the chart.

Look at a daily chart of any legit blue-chip stock, and you will notice some patterns to the movement. Of course each one will have a different look, but the point is, the movements won't look *chaotic*. Now look at the daily chart of a penny stock. It looks like an EKG of somebody having a stroke. No structure, wild up & down swings, huge gaps from day to day.

How are you supposed to to read charts like that with any level of predictability? You can't. It's like the difference between an expert card-counter in Vegas playing Blackjack vs. some first-timer tourist putting it all on 00 at the roulette table. Pro traders want to **minimize risk and maximize predictability.** There are many ways you can do both of these things, and the further along you get into your trading journey, the better you'll be able to do this.

So now that you realize you do NOT need to keep up on the latest news from a zillion different tickers, and you only need to trade a handful of blue-chip stocks *(whew!)* then WHAT exactly are you supposed to be looking for as you study the charts?

You're looking at Japanese candlesticks, and more importantly, you're interpreting the patterns those candlesticks form.

WHAT TO LOOK FOR

OK—you have your hardware and software set up, you've learned the basics of how your trading software works, you've figured out how your indicators work, you know what a candlestick is… you know what you're looking AT, but exactly what are you looking FOR?

First, you're looking for patterns that create trends—and then you're looking for confirmation of the validity and strength of those trends once the trends are established.

First I'm going to first talk about the patterns that create trends, and then I'm going to discuss how you put different pieces of information together in order to confirm the strength of those trends.

1. PATTERNS THAT CREATE TRENDS

There are many different patterns that develop from Japanese candlesticks, and I'm not going to get into all of them, only the most important ones. Mainly I'm looking for patterns that develop from groups of candlesticks, but there are also individual candlesticks that can provide tells.

But before I even get into Japanese candlestick patterns, I need to talk about the nature of the individual candlestick itself. Each candlestick represents the price movement of an asset over a specific time period (*for example, when you're viewing the one minute chart, each candlestick represents one minute of price action),* and Candlesticks consist of two main parts: the body and the wicks *(also known as shadows or tails).* Here's why both the bodies and the wicks are important.

Candlestick Body:

The body of the candlestick represents the range between the opening and closing prices of the asset during the specified time period. It is often filled *(colored)* or hollow *(empty)* based on whether the closing price is lower or higher than the opening price, respectively. So the body represents the *actual* opening and closing price for that specific time period. The length of the body indicates the degree of price movement during the time period. A longer body signifies significant price changes, while a shorter body indicates smaller price fluctuations.

If we see a chart with a lot of very small-bodied candles all close to the same price level, and the direction is mainly chugging along in a horizontal direction *(no noticeable upwards or downwards pressure)* then we have very little *trend.* It means the opening and closing prices of each period are very similar, and the overall direction is sideways *(consolidation).* Of course there are ways to make money trading this type of price action, but not with MY way of trading… so this scenario is the worst thing I can see. I stay out of the market when the price action looks like this.

On the other hand, if you see a chart with a lot of big-bodied candles all trending in either a bullish or bearish direction *(going up or down)*, this means there is a lot of trending pressure, and that's when I'd look for a slight pullback, which would be a good place to enter and ride the trend.

If you're looking to ride an established, continuing trend, large bodied candles with small or no wicks are what you want to see. Large wicks on candles signify more of a 'fight' taking place between the bulls & bears.

Candlestick Wicks:

Candlestick wicks are the thin lines that extend above and below the body of the candlestick. They represent the price range between the high and low prices achieved during the time period. The upper wick *(upper 'shadow' or 'tail')* extends from the top of the body to the high price. It indicates the highest price reached during the time period. The lower wick *(lower 'shadow' or 'tail')* extends from the bottom of the body to the low price. It indicates the lowest price reached during the time period.

Why are wicks important? Because while bodies represent the *actual* highs and lows of the period, wicks represent the *attempted* highs and lows of the period. This can be a telling visual, especially if we're looking at a trend that's running out of steam. For example, if a stock is trending bearish, falling hard, with a lot of solid red, long-bodied candles, and then suddenly we see a much shorter red candle with a long lower wick followed by a green candle, that could mean the bearish pressure is weakening or is ready to reverse. Price *tried* to go lower but failed *(hence the long lower wick)*.

Everything you see on the chart *means something*—your job is to figure out exactly *what* it means, and profit off of that meaning.

Together, candlestick bodies and wicks offer a visual representation of price dynamics and market sentiment that's extremely powerful once you know what to look for. By analyzing the relationship between the opening, closing, high, and low prices of candlesticks, both individually and in patterns, you can have more confidence about when to enter and exit your positions.

PATTERNS OF BEHAVIOR

OK, now that we've covered the actual candles, let's build off of our bodies/wicks knowledge and talk about individual and group candlestick patterns, and how these patterns are the code language that tells you where price *should* go next.

One such individual candlestick pattern is a doji, which is a candlestick that looks like a PLUS sign (+), and this results from the market's indecision. There's no real body, just upper and lower wicks—and this means that the market can't make up it's mind whether it wants to move up or down. It's important to use context when viewing individual candles.

Here's what I mean: if the price on the 1 minute chart has been steadily rising, with very long-bodied green candles, and then the bodies get progressively smaller minute-by-minute *(meaning upwards pressure is losing momentum)*, and *then* we see a doji candle, that's a pretty good sign that the upwards trend has lost momentum. At this point we could be due for a reversal.

To put this in context: imagine bouncing a ball off the ground. At first we'll have a strong rebounding force propelling the ball up in the air right after it hits the floor, and then the force will weaken as the ball comes up and pushes against the force of gravity. The exact moment when the ball is still in the air, but not moving up *or* down— metaphorically speaking, that's a doji candle.

Still using this doji example, if you view the same ticker on the same 1 minute chart, but price has just been consolidating *(moving sideways)* rather than rising, and all of the candles have similarly sized bodies, that same doji candle has less meaning, because there's no real *trend* for that doji candle to affect. This is what I mean by 'using context' whenever we look at individual candles or patterns. One candlestick that means something very significant in one context is meaningless in a different context.

Above we see an example of how a doji can have added 'meaning' when you don't just see the shape, but consider it's position in relation to the candles around it, and also it's relation to certain price levels. This is a 1 hour chart on AAPL, and you can see how this doji sits at a 'peak' right at the 200 EMA. The 200 EMA is significant because here it acts as a resistance level. Price was climbing, but then it ran into the 200 EMA, bounced off of it, and then fell.

This exact same highlighted candle would have held far less significance if it were in the middle of a consolidation, or if it were not sitting at any relevant price levels. All patterns are not created equal. It's important to see not only the shape of the candlestick, but everything that's happening *around* the candlestick.

There are plenty of other individual or 2-3 candlestick patterns that can help you identify trends, but a lot of these patterns are more useful for longer time frames *(more suitable for swing traders)*. For example, a bullish or bearing engulfing pattern *(when a candle is followed by a larger candle of opposite momentum that engulfs it)* is much more substantial on a daily chart than in the middle of a 1 minute chart that shows no real trend. Again, context is everything.

Even though there are lots of individual and 2-3 candlestick patterns you could learn, I'm only going to focus on the most important ones in relation to my style of day trading. These patterns take a bit longer to develop, typically 15 minutes or more on the 1 minute chart.

The MOST important pattern to look for on the 1 minute chart is the double top / double bottom

Remember the 'bouncing ball' example we were just talking about? That's the heart of the double top / double bottom pattern. In essence, a DT/DB is saying, *"This is the ceiling" (or floor)*. This is the level that price doesn't want to break through. So for a double bottom the pattern looks like the letter 'W' and a double top looks like the letter 'M'.

You can see the distinct 'W' and 'M' shapes in the image above. In hindsight, we could have made money going in either direction. If we opened a long position at the right side of the W *(double bottom)* and held it until we saw confirmation at the right side of the M *(double top)* we would have made money. Likewise, if we missed the double bottom but spotted the double top, we could have opened a short position at the right side of the M and rode it all the way down, taking profits along the way until we see a sign that the bearish pressure has weakened.

And the BEST possible scenario: If you were extremely observant & motivated, you could have played BOTH sides of the trade, getting in long at the right side of the double bottom, selling at the right side of the double top, and then entering short right afterwards. I don't usually do that type of thing, because I'm happy to just catch the move going in one direction... but you *could* do it if you felt like being a Ninja.

- Higher High / Lower Low

An even stronger variation of the DT/DB is the higher high & lower low. The only difference here is that the right side of the DT or DB is even higher or lower than the left side, which can give you even more confidence in the strength of the movement.

- The Bull/Bear Flag pattern

A bull or bear flag pattern is a continuation pattern characterized by a brief consolidation phase that occurs after a strong upward or downward price movement (*flagpole*), followed by a resumption of the trend. The bull flag pattern is named for its visual resemblance to a flag on a flagpole.

Here's how the flag pattern works:

- Flagpole *(the trend):* The pattern starts with a strong and rapid price movement up or down. This is known as the flagpole.

- Consolidation Phase *(the flag):* After the flagpole, the price enters a consolidation phase, forming a rectangular or parallelogram-shaped pattern that resembles a flag. This phase is characterized by relatively lower trading volume and sideways price movement. It's like a 'mini exhaustion' of the strong up or downward movement that was just happening.

- Breakout and Resumption of initial trend: The key feature of the flag pattern is the breakout from the flag pattern in the same direction as the initial trend. When the price breaks above the upper boundary of the flag pattern, it signals a potential continuation of the previous upward trend, and if price breaks below the lower boundary of the flag pattern, it signals a potential continuation of the previous downward trend.

The flag pattern *(bullish or bearish)* is a visual representation of a temporary pause in momentum before the price continues with that momentum. It's important to note that not all flag-like patterns are valid flags, so when you see what you *think* is a flag pattern, cross-reference it with the volume chart and RSI.

2. CONFIRMATION OF THE STRENGTH OF THE TREND

Once you have confirmed that a valid trend has developed, the next step is making sure that the trend is actually strong. This can be done in a number of ways. Here are some of the things I look at when attempting to calculate the strength of a trend:

- Price Movement and Volatility: Interpreting price movement correctly on your charts is the single best way to predict the strength of any trend. A strong trend is characterized by consistent price movement in one direction, with limited retracements or pullbacks. Higher volatility, as indicated by larger price swings, often accompanies strong trends. We've already established that the candlesticks are the 'bread and butter' we use in our trading—so obviously the first thing we do when trying to determine the strength of a trend is study the patterns created by the candlesticks.

The main reason I use multiple time frames and both Japanese and Heiken Ashi candlesticks on my charts is to have multiple options of price action to examine. If you only look at one chart one way, you only have that one particular bit of information to consider. But by having multiple time frames & representations of price action to consider, we broaden the scope of information we can use before we make trading decisions.

When I'm looking at the detail of the candlestick pattern, obviously I want to see a 'trending' direction *(bullish if I'm going long or bearish if I'm going short)* but there is nuance to the direction. Not all moves are created equally. My favorite type of direction is controlled and predictable. I like seeing candles that are all approximately the same size, trending in a steady movement—not looking like they're falling off a cliff or launching through the ceiling.

Those wildly dramatic movements are referred to as 'parabolic' moves. These moves look extremely jarring to the eye, and they can make you LOTS of money in just a few minutes if they're going in the right direction. But the problem is: moves like this can't be sustained. Whenever I'm in a position and a parabolic move goes in my favor, I *always* sell most if not *all* of my position at that moment, because you can be sure that type of directional movement won't last forever.

Here's a good rule of thumb to remember: If you're in a position and the trend is slow and steady in your favor, sell your contracts slowly as the trend develops. Sell one contract, wait…. sell one contract, wait… sell one contract, wait… and so on, until you see the strength of the trend starting to dissipate—at that point you should unload the rest of your contracts before the price action turns against you.

On the other hand, if a parabolic move happens in your favor, sell a larger chunk *(if not all)* of your position right when the move happens. That huge move will give you a spike in the options premium, and therefore it's best to capitalize on that surge in price action by closing out a larger chunk of your positions at once.

Simply studying price movement, noticing the size of the candles *(bodies and wicks)* and the directional arc of the candles is the best way to determine trend strength, but there are plenty of other pieces of information that can help you make profitable trading decisions, including:

- Moving Averages: The angle and separation of moving averages can indicate trend strength. A steeply rising or falling moving average with significant separation from another moving average can suggest a strong trend.

- Trend lines: The steepness of a trend line can provide clues about trend strength. A trend line with a steep angle indicates a stronger trend compared to a shallow-angle trend line.

- RSI (Relative Strength Index): While RSI is primarily used to identify overbought and oversold conditions, it can also help gauge trend strength. If RSI remains consistently in overbought or oversold territory, it suggests a strong trend. I change my RSI settings from the default of 70/30 to 80/20. I find this gives me less 'fake outs' and more predictability.

- Volume Analysis: Increasing trading volume during a price movement indicates higher market participation and potentially a stronger trend. More volume=more participation=more validity of the trend.

- MACD (Moving Average Convergence Divergence): The MACD histogram's size and steepness can indicate the strength of a trend. A widening histogram suggests increasing momentum and trend strength. When the green or red upper/lower histogram increases and the MACD line grows further apart from the slow line, that means the trend is strong.

- ADX (Average Directional Index): ADX is an indicator that measures the strength of a trend, regardless of its direction. A high ADX value suggests a strong trend, while a low value indicates a weak or ranging market. I don't keep this indicator on my charts full-time, but occasionally I'll pull it up to see if a strong ADX number confirms what I'm seeing from other sources.

I've just explained what we're looking for as we try to identify patterns, but it's even easier to describe what we DON'T want to see. Here it is:

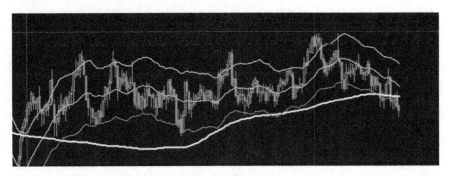

Run away as fast as you can from a chart that looks like this. There is NO trend. Price is just moving sideways. With my strategy, we never make money when price is consolidating. As I've said before, it IS possible to make money on chart like this, but not the way I trade. I want to see very strong trends in either direction.

You can see the *possible* beginnings of a bearish trend starting to form in the last 10-15 candles due to the lower highs being formed *(also notice the downward slope of the Keltner Channels)*, but if I were watching this chart I would wait until the mid-line of the Keltner Channels crossed below the 200 EMA, and then I might start in small with a short position. But I certainly wouldn't touch anything in the middle of this image unless I was looking to scalp trade, which is something I rarely do.

Now that we've covered most of the 'basic information' you'll need to get started, I'm going to teach you about options—including the right strike prices to take, expiration dates, etc. Remember, as you continue on this journey—if there's anything you read about that you'd like further explanation on, feel free to put the book down and do some research elsewhere, then come back and pick up where you left off.

Day trading is a topic that contains SO MUCH potential information, there's no way that any one book can teach you everything you could know about the stock market. It's like reading one book about brain surgery and then thinking you know everything about the human brain. But I do promise you I'll teach you everything you need to know about how to effectively use *my* strategy by the time you've finished this book.

CHAPTER 8

The Process

"Many of life's failures are people who did not realize how close they were to success when they gave up." — Thomas A. Edison

In this chapter we're going to discuss some common pitfalls novice traders make and learn how to avoid them. I'll get into the specifics of how to enter, manage and exit trades in the next few chapters. For now, I'll continue with a high-level overview of my strategy so it can really sink in before you get into actually making trades.

Hopefully I've already made this crystal clear, but for the sake of repetition let me reiterate—**the way I trade is to identify a trend, hop on and take the ride**. When I receive confirmation that the trend is getting exhausted and could be near a reversal, I hop off. The concept really IS as simple as that. Now in *practice*, it's not always that simple at first—but with a keen eye, dedication and countless hours of studying price action, it *will* become that simple to you over time. The simplicity is real. This is ALL I DO. I trade ONE strategy, with just a small handful of stocks… and when my strategy is executed correctly, I am virtually guaranteed to make money every single day.

Of course there was a time when I was much less experienced *(and therefore less confident)*, but now I no longer ask myself, *"I wonder if I'll make money today?"* I ask myself, *"How much money will I make today?"* It might be $300, it might be $3,000. I don't even care anymore *exactly* how much I make each day, because I know I have a strategy that's practically bulletproof, one that allows me to use the market like my own personal ATM. All of my bills are paid, and I can buy whatever I want.

SWIM WITH THE CURRENT

What does it mean to 'swim with the current?' It means that more often than not, you'll find it an exercise in futility if you try to buck the trend. Imagine you're sitting on a raft in a gently moving stream. Is it easier for you to paddle against the current, or just relax and take the ride?

One of the most common mistakes novice traders make is choosing entries without any mature conformation that a trend or reversal is actually happening, therefore getting 'faked out' by a false breakout or reversal. I was absolutely guilty of this many times early on in my career. I would see a chart trending hard in a certain direction and think to myself,

"I've got a feeling it's about to reverse" only to get faked out because the reversal I 'felt' was about to happen DIDN'T happen *(the data on the charts didn't support my feeling).*

Remember this: FEELINGS are for relationships and emo bands. They have no place in trading. It's perfectly natural *(and un-avoidable)* to 'have a feeling' that a particular thing is about to happen, but DO NOT TRADE based upon that feeling. **Trade the chart, not your feelings.**

Another novice mistake is to NOT get into a trade simply because you missed the first candle of the move. This is silly. Would you rather capture 60% of a move, or not take the trade at all because you were too late to capture 90% of the move? Gains are gains. 6%, 23%, 57%… ALL gains are good gains. Of course there comes a point when it really IS too late to responsibly enter the trade. If the stock has already been making big moves for the last 30 minutes, you may not capture any meaningful gains *(unless you're playing with HUGE size and taking more of a scalp approach).* I identify the *beginning* of the trend, but I don't get hung up on the need to get in on the *first* candle.

Yet another amateur mistake is buying FAR out of the money options and hoping for a home run. The novice trader is fooled into thinking that's a good idea simply because the options are cheap. That approach is more like gambling than professional trading.

LOOK, THEN TOUCH, THEN DEVOUR

You've already got your computer, monitor & brokerage software all set up. You know which tickers you're going to focus on, and you've studied 'the basics'... so you're *almost* ready to trade.

But don't get ahead of yourself. I don't want you jumping into trades with size until you're absolutely ready. And what I mean by 'absolutely ready' is... I want you to do nothing but watch the charts for at least a few weeks *(or even months if you need to)* before moving on to actually trading for real. How will you know when you're ready to trade with real money? When you start to understand more often than not *why* the charts look like they do.

Remember, you will NEVER have a complete understanding of everything that happens in the market. Even now, after years of trading I'll still find myself confounded by unexplained moves in price action, and I'm sure people with decades more trading experience than me also get surprised regularly.

There have been many times I've analyzed price action, and every signal I pick up tells me one thing will happen... but then something completely different happens. That's just the nature of the beast. As I've already stated, **THE MARKET WILL DO WHAT IT WANTS, WHENEVER IT WANTS.**

But that's OK... we will still make money, even knowing this fact. Being right 70% of the time is nothing to scoff at.

THE PAPER TRADING QUESTION

In case you don't already know—paper trading in stock options, also known as simulated or virtual trading, refers to the practice of trading options without using real money. Instead of executing actual trades with real capital, traders use a simulated environment to place trades, track their performance, and learn about the options market. Many trading programs have a paper trading feature (*including Think Or Swim*).

Lots of traders are quick to espouse the benefits of paper trading, but I am not one of them. I'm not *against* paper trading per se, but here's my problem with it: it's not REAL. Even if you're paper trading with roughly the same size as you would with real money, your psychology won't work the same way. Dealing with imaginary money is simply different than dealing with REAL money.

Of course there are educational benefits to learning the process of actually placing the trade. Selecting your strikes & expiation dates, and getting familiar with which buttons to click at which times. The act of physically going through the steps without risking real money is helpful.

My advice to you is this: spend a LOT of time simply watching the charts and observing price action, then spend a SMALL amount of time paper trading *(just enough until you get used to the process of executing a trade)* and then spend a LOT of days trading ONE contract per day. For your first few months *(at least)* on your trading journey, give yourself a '1 contract per day' limit and stick to it. This is good for a number of reasons. The first and most obvious reason is simply for the repetitions and the practice. But I can't over-emphasize how important it is to build a sense of *discipline* in your mind when it comes to trading.

Like I said a few chapters back: trading will teach you more about yourself than just about anything else you could do. This is where you will truly discover how much mental discipline you possess. If you discover that you don't have enough mental discipline to keep yourself from going 'all in' at every opportunity, that's a big problem that needs to be addressed NOW and not later.

It's so easy to over trade, or to 'revenge trade' *(trying to get back a previous loss with a new trade).* You don't want to do any of this. You simply want to plot your support & resistance lines for the day, observe the candlestick patterns on the chart, get into the trade at the right time based on the strategy, and then get out of the trade at the right time based on the strategy. Don't let feelings of greed or revenge or fear cloud your judgement.

ALL ABOUT STRIKES AND EXPIRATIONS

Before you can buy a call or put option, you need to decide two things: the strike price and the expiration date you want to purchase. Strike prices play a crucial role in stock options, as they determine the price at which the underlying stock can be bought or sold if the option is exercised. When you trade options, you are essentially making a contract that gives you the right *(but not the obligation)* to buy or sell the underlying stock at a specific strike price on or before the option's expiration date.

First I'll take you through what the price chart looks like from a visual perspective, then I'll explain what it all means. When you look at the options strike price chart for the first time, you'll probably say to yourself, *"WTF.... I can't make sense of that much information."* Well guess what, I have great news! You only need to pay attention to about 5% of all the information in this screenshot.

Here's what today's SPY chart looks like on TOS.

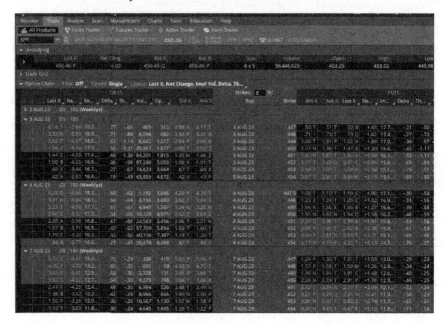

As you can see, we have a LEFT side of the chart, a RIGHT side, and a middle column. The section in the middle tells you 2 things: the amount of days till expiration of that particular contract you choose (EXP), and the strike prices available (STRIKE). In the left column we can see prices for CALL options, and in the right column we see prices for PUT options.

So according to this chart at the exact moment I took the screenshot, a person could buy a call option with a 450 strike price that expired on 08/03/23 for $202 (*$2.02 per share X 100 shares that 1 options contract contains*). If you gave yourself 1 extra day of time value and bought the same 450 strike price call option, that option would cost you $263. And if you gave yourself 4 extra days by purchasing that same 450 strike but with a 08/07/23 expiration, that option will cost you $306.

This illustrates how the old adage 'time is money' really is true. The more time you give yourself to expiration, the more expensive the option will cost, because more time until expiration means more time for your option to expire *in the money,* which is what you want.

You can see in the middle column that I have the amount of strike prices I'm viewing set to 8 *(Strikes: 8).* You can set this to show as many strikes as you want to see, but I keep mine set to 8 because I almost never go further away from an "at the money" strike price.

So what IS 'at the money', you ask?

- At-the-money (ATM) options have strike prices very close to the stock's market price. In the example here we can see that at the exact moment I took this screenshot, SPY was trading at 450.46 *(the green number to the right of the SPY ticker symbol at the top of the chart).*

- In-the-money (ITM) options have intrinsic value and are closer to the stock's market price.

- Out-of-the-money (OTM) options have no intrinsic value and are further from the stock's market price.

This may look complicated at first glance, but it's not that hard to understand. Here's how strike prices work:

Call Options and Strike Prices:

In call options, the holder *(buyer)* has the right to buy the underlying stock at the strike price. When you buy a call option, you are paying for the right to purchase the stock at the strike price, regardless of the stock's current market price. If the stock's market price rises above the strike price, the call option becomes more valuable, as you can buy the stock at a lower price than the current market price.

Put Options and Strike Prices:

In put options, the holder *(buyer)* has the right to sell the underlying stock at the strike price. When you buy a put option, you are paying for the right to sell the stock at the strike price, regardless of the stock's current market price. If the stock's market price falls below the strike price, the put option becomes more valuable, as you can sell the stock at a higher price than the current market price.

Intrinsic Value and Strike Prices:

The difference between the current market price of the underlying stock and the strike price determines the intrinsic value of an option.

- For call options, if the stock's market price is above the strike price, the option has intrinsic value. The higher the market price above the strike, the greater the intrinsic value.

- For put options, if the stock's market price is below the strike price, the option has intrinsic value. The higher the strike price above the market price, the greater the intrinsic value.

The expiration date:

As I just mentioned, the more time you have until expiration, the more expensive the contract will be. This is because every options contract contains both time value and intrinsic value. Time decay starts melting down the value of your contract(s) from the moment you open the position. This is why I never trade with a same-day expiration. ETF's like SPY and QQQ allow you to buy contracts that expire every day of the week from Monday through Friday.

AVOID THE ASSIGNMENT

If you fail to close an options contract before its expiration date, the outcome depends on whether the option is in-the-money (ITM), at-the-money (ATM), or out-of-the-money (OTM). Here's what can happen in each scenario:

- In-the-Money (ITM) Options:

It's important to close your ITM options contracts before they expire, because you *don't* want to be 'assigned.' What does this mean? If you hold an ITM call option and it's not closed or exercised before expiration, your brokerage may automatically exercise the option on your behalf. This means they'll buy the underlying asset at the strike price for you.

If this does happen to you, it's not the end of the world. I once accidentally held some ITM call options on FB *(back when it was still called Facebook)* past expiration, and woke up the next day to realize I had been *assigned*, so at that point I *owned* shares of FB, which I did NOT want... I only wanted to trade the *options* on FB.

The solution is simple- just sell the underlying shares the next day, as soon as you find an advantageous time to do so. You'll no longer own any shares, and you'll have freed up the capital to keep on trading options, which is what you wanted to do in the first place.

- At-the-Money (ATM) Options:

If you hold an ATM option that expires, your brokerage may automatically exercise the option, but the outcome depends on the direction of the option *(call or put)* and market conditions at that moment.

- Out-of-the-Money (OTM) Options:

If you hold an OTM option and it's not closed or exercised before expiration, your brokerage will likely let the option expire worthless. In this case, you won't take any further action, and the option will disappear from your account. At that point, you would have lost the entire price you paid for the options contract(s).

It's important to understand your brokerage's policies regarding options expiration and exercise. Some brokers have default settings to automatically exercise certain ITM options, while others require traders to give explicit instructions. Always consult your broker's terms and conditions and understand their procedures for handling expiring options. Remember: if you do not want to exercise or have your options automatically exercised, **it's always crucial to close your options positions before the expiration date.**

So now that you understand strike prices and expiration dates, it's time to look for entries.

CHAPTER 9

Entries

"The common man is not concerned about the passage of time, the man of talent is driven by it." — Arthur Schopenhauer

I have already explained how my screens are set up, and what I do to prepare between 8AM and the opening of the market. Once the market opens and I start trading — if everything goes perfectly then I'm completely out of all positions by 10 AM (CST). Sometimes I will hold a position open for a few hours or even until the afternoon if I'm trying to squeeze a bit more out of my trade, OR if I'm looking for an afternoon reversal because the trade has gone against me during the morning session *(it does happen occasionally).*

You'll need to develop a sense of nuance about *exactly* when to get in after the market opens each day. What I mean is: I've said that I like to get in as soon as possible each day, but that doesn't mean hit the BUY button the second you hear the opening bell. Usually, volatility is at it's highest point of the day during the first hour of trading, and we can use that to our advantage—but be very careful during the first 5-10 minutes, because a lot of stop orders will automatically trigger first thing in the morning due to gaps that happened overnight.

Also, some institutional traders *(the people who REALLY move the market)* haven't arrived at work yet, so the 'smart money' hasn't really started to influence price action until at least 10 minutes in. I do frequently open positions within the first 5 minutes of the open, but when I do, normally I'll keep my size small and wait to see if my initial suspicions were correct. If they were, then I'll hit my position with larger size after 10-15 minutes has elapsed, once I have more confirmation that the move is actually real and not a fake out, or simply the result of stop orders moving the price *(which will happen in the first few minutes of the day)*.

IN A NUTSHELL, THIS IS THE THREE STEP TRADING STRATEGY I USE EVERY DAY:

1. Check the daily chart to identify any significant support/resistance lines, and look for any significant candlestick patterns that give me a bullish or bearish lean.

2. Observe the 200 and 50 EMA's, and see where price sits in relation to both of them. Is the 50 above or below the 200? Are they trending up or down? If the price, Alligator and both EMA's are all 'stacked' in one

direction *(either bullish or bearish)* that's a very strong trending signal.

3. Get confirmation from the volume chart, RSI and MACD that the trend is 'real.' Once I am satisfied by the level of confirmation I see, I'll look for a slight pullback in price action to get into the trade.

You already know the different time frames we'll view on our charts *(1-minute, 15 minute, 30 minute, 1 hour)* but where should your eyes actually be focused as you trade? REMEMBER THIS:

WE *ONLY* LOOK AT THE 1-MINUTE CHART FOR ENTRIES *AND* EXITS

All three of our intraday time frames are valid for identifying the formation and confirmation of trends, but the 1-minute chart is the ONLY chart you should look at as you enter and exit the trade.

If your hand is on the mouse, your eyes should be on the 1-minute chart.

Why is this true? Because price can fluctuate WILDLY from second to second. Attempting to enter or exit even on a 5 minute chart allows for wayyyy too much price fluctuation. When you look at a 1-minute candle, you can see the price moving in real time with each passing second. For example: if you're looking to go long and you've identified the pullback zone where you want to enter, the second that candle wick touches the level you're comfortable with, you click the 'buy' button—and as long as you've placed a market order *(and as long as you have a fast connection)* you should get your order filled immediately, very close to the price you expected to pay.

Remember that each individual candlestick on each time frame represents price action during that period—so a 1-minute candle represents 60 seconds worth of trading activity, 30 minutes represents 30 minutes of activity, etc. So obviously, the closer you get to seeing the *immediate*, real time price of the stock on the candlestick, the more accurate you will be on your entries and exits.

Here's one more thing about time frames that I should clarify before getting into interpreting patterns: while the moving averages being 'stacked' in the right direction is very important when we're looking for entries on the 1-minute chart, it's less important to see that stacked pattern on the 30 minute chart. Here's why. When we enter into any position, we're looking to capitalize on the *immediacy* of the price action. What this means is: we're not really worrying about what price did 30 minutes ago, we're thinking about what price is doing *right* now.

Mature reversals can *definitely* develop within a 30 minute time frame, so it's very possible to see that the most recent 30 minute candle is red even though a strong bullish reversal has already formed. That's why the 1 minute chart is the most important chart in day trading. Longer term charts are definitely useful to cross reference simply as additional pieces of information, but the 1-minute is your go-to chart in day trading when you're trying to get in and out within 1 hour.

During premarket *(before the market opens)* the Daily chart is the most important chart to look at, since premarket is the time when we look for significant levels, plot daily trends and identify daily candlestick patterns. All of these things will greatly help us know what to look for once the market opens up. This is what I mean when I talk about *leaning* long or short for the day. Basically, I'll interpret a lot of visual information from the daily chart before the market opens, and that information will make me say, *"This looks like it's setting up to be a green day"* (or a red day, depending on what I see).

This next bit is SUPER important. Just because you're *leaning* a certain direction based on what you see on the daily chart during premarket—that doesn't guarantee anything. I have experienced many days when premarket has 'told me' one thing based on my daily chart analysis, but then as soon as the market opens, it does the opposite. When this happens, you just need to be nimble and be able to adapt to quickly changing conditions.

It's OK to go long *(or short)* right at the beginning of the day based on your premarket technical analysis, but then flip direction as soon as you see a mature trend developing in the opposite direction once the market opens. The key here is to make sure it's a *mature trend* developing in the opposite direction before you get out and get back in. Don't just blindly flip-flop long & short 10 times a day because you're afraid of taking the ride and letting the trend work. If you flip-flop all day, it will inevitably lead to OVERTRADING. Plenty of traders overtrade. It's easy to do, and it can be costly.

How do you know if you're overtrading? Here's an example: If you enter a long position, and then close it out on the first few red candles because you're afraid to lose any money—and then you open a short position *before* you see a mature bearish trend developing—and then you close *that* position out with the first few green candles you see…. That's overtrading. It's a 'rinse and repeat' cycle of getting out too early because you're afraid to let it work.

If you do a good job of identifying the right time to enter, whether it's long or short, you should have at least 20-40 minutes of trend you can ride before the trend stalls or a reversal happens, and often you can ride it even longer. It's very rare that any stock will trend in the same direction *all day* without the trend losing steam or reversing, but even that does happen sometimes.

The key to my strategy is: **GET IN AS CLOSE AS POSSIBLE TO THE START OF A TREND, AND GET OUT AS CLOSE AS POSSIBLE TO THE END OF THAT TREND.** If you become proficient at doing JUST those two things, you WILL be successful doing this.

OK, back to candles. I *always* make the most important intraday decisions based on the 1 minute candles. The other time frames are important as additional pieces of information and can help confirm the strength and 'lifespan' of a trend, but 1 minute candles are *by far* the most important thing a day trader should be looking at when the market is open. Think about this in Hollywood blockbuster terms. The 1 minute candle is Tom Cruise, and the other time frames represent everyone else in a Tom Cruise movie.

To summarize this part... here's a quick & easy way to remember what to focus on *(and when)* each day:

- PREMARKET: **The daily chart is the most important one. Use this to identify valid daily support & resistance levels and plot trends.**

- DURING TRADING HOURS: **The 1 minute chart is the most important one. Use this to determine the correct entry & exit points.**

INTERPRETING THE PRICE + EMA's

One of the fundamental aspects of my strategy is looking at the relationship of the candlesticks to the EMA's (50 + 200) and then making decisions based on that information PLUS what I see on my other indicators. There are a few different ways the price action + EMA's can be aligned, and that alignment will show us bullish or bearish pressure in relationship to the passage of time. Here are a few examples.

- CANDLESTICKS>50 EMA>200 EMA: This is the most bullish combination. With the candlesticks being above the 50 *(shorter term price action)*, which is itself above the 200 *(longer term price action)*, this shows us that everything is trending up. Short term, long term, and immediate price action *(because of the candlesticks being above everything)*.

- CANDLESTICKS<50 EMA<200 EMA: This is the most bearish combination. It's the above example but in reverse. In this example, everything is 'stacked' to the downside.

- CANDLESTICKS>50 EMA<200 EMA: When the candlesticks are above the 50 EMA, but the 50 is below the 200 EMA, this can mean one of two things. Either a bear flag *(a slight reversal of bearish pressure before the downward trend continues)* or the start of a reversal. Remember, all reversals start by creating a divergence between the longer & shorter term trend. The longer term trend is going in one direction, but the shorter term trend is going in the other direction. This is yet another reason why simply looking at one timeframe on one chart won't work. You'll need to view price action and your indicators on multiple charts, and then decide which data seems most valid.

- CANDLESTICKS<50 EMA>200 EMA: As with the first 2 examples, this is essentially the same as the example above but in reverse. When you see candles below the 50 but the 50 is above the 200, we're probably seeing either a bull flag or the beginning of a reversal. It's up to you to check multiple sources of information on multiple charts to determine which scenario is most likely, and act accordingly.

- CANDLESTICKS=50 EMA=200 EMA: This is when you DON'T want to trade. Go back to the image in chapter 7 for an example of what consolidating price action looks like. When everything is basically chugging along on a horizontal line, that means price is consolidating and *not* trending strongly in either direction. The only thing happening here is that time *(Theta)* decay is eating away at your options premium. Remember, Theta decay starts the second you open your position.

One final note about candlesticks and their relationship to the EMA's: The raw data you see on the charts are the 'puzzle pieces' and your mind is the thing that puts all of those pieces together, in order to see the big picture. This is where your skill is essential. Anyone could essentially flip a coin that told them whether to go long or short or long that day and be right 50% of the time, but having the skill to make sense of everything you see will be the difference between continued success or failure.

There's no 'one thing' to look for, and that's why it can be so scary to beginning traders. But trust me: just keep doing it, and you WILL get it. It took me years before I was actually confident in what I was doing. But once that confidence really sets in, it never goes away. I am 100% confident that if anyone gave me 2K I could turn that into at least 8K by the end of 1 month. And that's a beautiful feeling to have.

INTERPRETING THE PATTERNS

Before I enter into a trade, I want to make sure a lot of things check out. Studying the charts and doing my research into price action and pattern formation *before* I open the trade is an essential part of the process. NOT doing these things is like taking a school exam without studying first, or going on a camping trip without bringing a tent. They simply MUST be done if you want any chance of success.

We've discussed the characteristics of individual candlesticks *(the body and the wick)*, and the relationship of our 2 EMA's to price action. We've also discussed how you should view multiple time frames on your charts, but the real 'bread and butter' of successful trading lies in acting upon the patterns you see that develop from interpreting multiple candlesticks together on your chart.

Candlestick patterns are formations that provide insights into potential price movements. We use these patterns to identify trends, reversals, and possible entry and exit points for our trades. Back in step one when I said, *"Look for any significant candlestick patterns that give me a bullish or bearish lean"* this is what I was talking about.

Here are some of the most important candlestick patterns:

- Double Top: The double top pattern is a bearish reversal pattern that occurs after an uptrend. It signifies that a trend reversal might be imminent. It consists of two peaks *(high points)* on the price chart that are roughly at the same level, with a trough *(low point)* between them. The pattern suggests that after the second peak, buyers are no longer able to push the price higher, and selling pressure could lead to a downtrend. This pattern looks like the letter 'M.'

- Double Bottom: The double bottom pattern is a bullish reversal pattern that occurs after a downtrend. It indicates a potential trend reversal. It consists of two troughs *(low points)* on the price chart that are approximately at the same level, with a peak *(high point)* between them. The pattern suggests that after the second trough, sellers are losing momentum, and buying pressure could lead to an uptrend. This pattern looks like the letter 'W.'

- Doji: A doji occurs when the open and close prices are very close or equal, resulting in a small or no real body. It indicates indecision in the market and can signal a potential trend reversal.

- Engulfing Patterns: An engulfing pattern occurs when one candlestick engulfs the previous one. A bullish engulfing pattern forms in a downtrend and can signal a reversal, while a bearish engulfing pattern forms in an uptrend and can indicate a potential reversal.

- Hammer: A hammer has a small real body near the top of the candlestick and a long lower shadow. It suggests potential bullish reversal after a downtrend.

- Shooting Star: The shooting star is the opposite of a hammer. It has a small real body near the bottom of the candlestick and a long upper shadow. It can signal a potential bearish reversal after an uptrend.

- Head and Shoulders: The head and shoulders pattern is a bearish reversal pattern that signifies a potential shift from an uptrend to a downtrend. It consists of three peaks: a higher peak *(the head)* between two lower peaks *(the shoulders)*, with a neckline connecting the troughs between the peaks. The neckline acts as a support level. When the price breaks below the neckline, it confirms the pattern and suggests a trend reversal. The head and shoulders pattern indicates that the buying momentum is weakening and sellers might take control.

- Inverse Head and Shoulders: The inverse head and shoulders pattern is a bullish reversal pattern that indicates a potential change from a downtrend to an uptrend. It is the opposite of the regular head and shoulders pattern. It consists of three troughs: a lower trough *(the head)* between two higher troughs *(the shoulders)*, with a neckline connecting the peaks between the troughs. When the price breaks above the neckline, it confirms the pattern and suggests a trend reversal. The inverse head and shoulders pattern indicates that selling pressure is weakening, and buyers might gain control.

I consider the above patterns to be the most important ones to look for, but there are others you can look out for, including:

- Harami: The harami pattern involves a small candlestick within the range of the previous larger candlestick. A bullish harami appears in a downtrend and can signal a reversal, while a bearish harami appears in an uptrend and can suggest a potential reversal.

- Morning Star: The morning star is a three-candle pattern. It starts with a bearish candle, followed by a small candle, and then a bullish candle. It indicates a potential reversal from a downtrend to an uptrend.

- Evening Star: The evening star is the opposite of the morning star. It starts with a bullish candle, followed by a small candle, and then a bearish candle. It suggests a potential reversal from an uptrend to a downtrend.

- Dark Cloud Cover: This bearish pattern consists of a bullish candle followed by a larger bearish candle that opens above the previous day's close and closes below its midpoint.

- Piercing Pattern: The piercing pattern is a bullish reversal pattern. It consists of a bearish candle followed by a bullish candle that opens below the previous day's close and closes above its midpoint.

- Bullish and Bearish Tweezer Patterns: These patterns involve two or more candlesticks with identical highs or lows, indicating potential reversals in price direction.

Here's something that's VERY important to remember: just because you see a pattern forming, that doesn't mean you should take the trade based on the pattern alone. **CONFIRMATION IS KEY.** We get confirmation by looking at chart patterns while cross-referencing them with our indicators to see if those patterns are valid or not.

Every day you'll see patterns that make you think a particular move is about to happen, but you *must* get confirmation by way of support & resistance levels and congruence with our indicators before you can have confidence the trade will work. The image below is a perfect example of what I'm talking about. Just take a look at the image before you read any further, and then see if you noticed any of the things I'm about to explain.

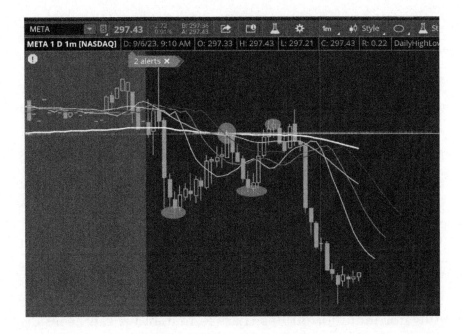

At first glance, what do you see? Based on the oval highlights, it'a a double bottom, right? The candlesticks are clearly making a 'W' shape, and the right side lows and highs are even higher than the left, so we should definitely go long here, right? Not so fast. Upon closer inspection, we see a few things that would definitely keep me from going long right here. First off, the main body of the 'W' is sitting below the 200 EMA, and the lows of the 'W' are sitting below the bottom of the Alligator.

The alignment of the indicators doesn't give me much confidence in a long position here. Although the Alligator is looking uncertain in the first four minutes, after the 9th or 10th minute of the day it dips below the 200 EMA, and the arc of the 200 EMA is sloping downwards, even if only slightly. Sure, this setup *could* break to the upside... but what I'm seeing here wouldn't get me in long just yet. In hindsight we can see that price *did* indeed break down hard just 5 minutes after the green doji sitting right above the 200 EMA. In order for me to get in long here, I'd need to see price break above the green candles we see at 3 minutes *before* the open. If that happened, I'd feel much more confident in a long position.

This is one of the many reasons why it's so important to get confirmation of your chart patterns by cross-referencing them with other indicators. If we took the 200 EMA and the Alligator indicator off this chart so that all we saw were the candlesticks, it would a bit easier to understand why someone would go long here. But with the addition of the 200 EMA and the Alligator, when you interpret all of this visual information as a whole and not as individual pieces, you should think twice before going long at this moment.

Speaking of visual information—It's extremely easy to get overloaded with too much visual information on your charts, and that's why I use a very limited amount of indicators. You can also go too far in the other direction—having NO indicators would make the process more difficult, as would having too many.

Think about it like cooking. If you were trying to make a pasta dish, and *all you had* were the noodles and nothing else, you already know how bland that would taste. But now imagine you made the same dish, but added literally EVERY spice in your pantry, and every sauce, and every ingredient… you'd have a convoluted mess of flavors that would be so overwhelming, you probably couldn't identify *any* flavor clearly. Moderation is key. Use just what you need, and nothing more.

THIS IS WHAT A GOOD ENTRY LOOKS LIKE

Take a look at this short entry on SPY. Here's the wide view

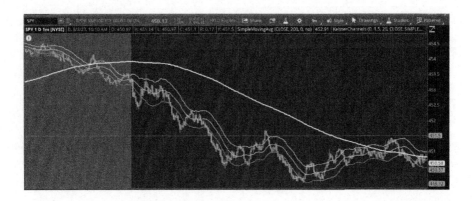

And here's the magnified view at the exact few minutes you should have entered the trade—8:45-8:46AM

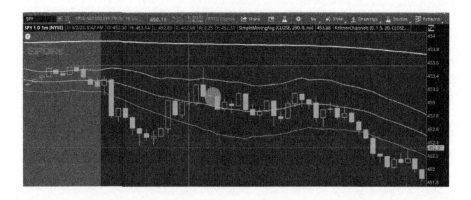

I bought a 454 strike price, which gave me approximately 1 point of insulation in case the price moved against me. Usually I like to give myself around 1 point of ITM protection—so in this case SPY was trading around 453, and I wanted to go short, so I bought the 454 put options— meaning I had the right to sell SPY for 454 per contract— which means I had 1 point of intrinsic value on that contract.

This trade alone got me around 3 points, which is a nice gain. Exactly how much profit or loss you'll accrue per point of price action movement depends on a few things, including volatility and the price of the underlying contract—but a 3 point move in your favor will always be a nice profit, even on inexpensive contracts. As a general rule, one point of movement should give you nice profits as long as you had a good entry. So obviously, a three point move is even better.

As you can see, this particular trade took a bit longer to develop, bit that's OK. You won't always have that perfectly convenient entry/exit setup where you get in 5 minutes after the market opens and you're out 15 minutes later.

THIS IS WHAT A BAD ENTRY LOOKS LIKE

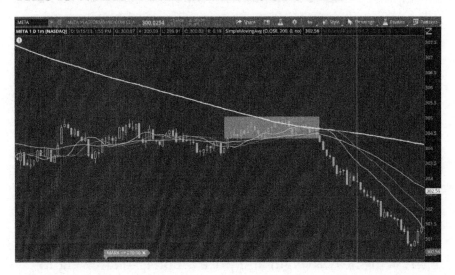

Take a look at the highlighted section of the META chart above. You might be tempted to go long here for a few reasons, like:

- Price is above the 50 EMA *and* the Alligator

- The Alligator's mouth is opening

- Price has made 2 higher lows

But going long at this moment is a bad idea, and here's why. We can see in the highlighted section that price is about to intersect with the 200 EMA, so you may be tempted to think, *"Price is going to slice through the 200 and then we'll rip higher."*

This is a classic case of jumping the gun, because if you take a closer look at the directional movement of both price action and the 200 EMA, you can see that price action is just chugging along horizontally, while the 200 is trending downwards at a pretty steep slope. The 200 is moving with force, while the price is just meandering with no purpose. It's no surprise that when these 2 forces intersect, the one that's moving with more strength will win.

It's like if two MMA fighters hit each other as hard as they can at exactly the same time, but one of them weighs 125 lbs. and the other one weighs 265 lbs. Which one do you think will get knocked out? The heavyweight is swinging with much more force than the flyweight. In this case, the 200 EMA is the heavyweight and price action is the flyweight.

As you can see, price rejected off of the 200 EMA as expected, and fell hard. If you would have waited until you saw price confidently break below the 50 EMA, you could have gone short right there and rode it for 25 minutes of solid gains. And if for some reason price did actually break *above* the 200 EMA, then you could have take a long position at that point with more confidence, knowing that the 200 EMA is such a substantial level.

IN SUMMARY

Here are the the 'must have' scenarios you'll need to see before entering any trade using my strategy:

BEFORE YOU GO LONG:

- The Alligator indicator and/or Keltner Channels needs to be ABOVE the 200 EMA and the 50 EMA on the 1-minute chart *(at the very least price needs to be above the 50 EMA)*. Preferably all of your visual information would be 'stacked' in the right direction.

- The candlesticks need to be firmly sitting in the top half of the Alligator Indicator or Keltner Channels *(between the mid line and the top line)*, OR, in the case of consolidating price action or a reversal, you need to see at least 3 candlesticks close ABOVE the top line before you can feel confident that a legitimate trend has developed.

- Study the visual of the trend lines on the Alligator Indicator and/or Keltner Channels. What is the angle of the slope? We want the upward slope to be as steep as possible. Ideally something like 40 degrees or more. A very slight upward slope reveals a much less aggressive trend than a steep slope, and of course we want the trend to be as aggressive as possible. Regarding the Alligator Indicator, the larger the space is between all three lines, the better it is for us *(as long as we're on the right side of it).* The reason it's called "The Alligator" is because the indicator resembles the mouth of an Alligator. When the lines are far apart the mouth is 'roaring', signifying a stronger trend in that direction.

BEFORE YOU GO SHORT:

It's exactly the same as above but reversed. So for example, you'd need the candlesticks and the Alligator Indicator/Keltner Channels to be BELOW the 200 EMA, the slope of the Alligator or Keltner to be moving DOWN, etc.

Although the things I just listed above are the most important pieces of information to consider before entering a trade, there are a number of 'nice to have' things that will help confirm the legitimacy of your trade idea, and give you even more confidence in taking the trade before you enter.

The 200 EMA on the 30 minute Heiken Ashi charts should be trending upwards. It's not as important that price action is ABOVE the 200 EMA on the 30 minute charts, because remember that longer time frames include more price discrepancy and the possibility of reversals forming. If price was down all day yesterday but has shot up within the last 30 minutes—price might still be below the 200 EMA on the 1 hour chart, but that doesn't mean it's not a good time to go long.

At the very least, wherever price actually sits on the 15 and 30 minute charts— at least make sure the 200 EMA is trending in the right direction.

If I were making a list of the 'most important' things to consider in the grand scheme of trading… there would be a lot of different things I'd mention. But **having great entries and exits is *literally* the most important thing you can do on a daily basis.** As with everything else, it will take time and practice, but you'll get there.

As I've said before *(and will say many more times in this book)* The concept of 'perfection' is really an illusion when it comes to trading. Even a GREAT entry or exit could always be a *little* better, had you gotten in or out a few seconds earlier or later… so don't get hung up on having 'the perfect' entry or exit. As long as you get in *close to* the start of the trend and get out *close to* the end of the trend, you'll do just fine.

CHAPTER 10

Managing the Trade

"Those who restrain desire do so because theirs is weak enough to be restrained." — William Blake

Being IN the trade *(with open contracts that you're watching develop minute-by-minute)* is the most intense part of the whole trading experience. This is literally the heart of the matter. It's the most dramatic and consequential part of everything. Making a great entry and exit is extremely important if you're only trading 1-3 contracts... but if you're trading with larger size, then managing the trade once you're *in it* is the MOST important aspect of your day.

We can make an analogy here comparing trading to some other fun & exciting thing... like going to the beach. Premarket study and technical analysis is like getting ready before you leave. Which swim suit will you wear? Which towel & bag should you take? Will you bring a cooler with you, or not? What time will you leave?

Once the day is over and you've returned from the beach, that's when you look at the photos you took that day or the seashells you collected. You contemplate your experience at the beach. This is like you studying the success or failure of your trading that day. What worked? What didn't work? WHY did you succeed or fail?

But when you're right there in the ocean, swimming, feeling the waves swirling all around you as you paddle your arms in the water.... That's actually *being in the trade.* This is the literal experience that you've planned for, the one you will remember and talk about later.

So now that you understand how important this actual part of the process is, what's the right way to manage the trade once you're opened your position? When should you close the trade? Should you sell all of your contracts at once, or should you peel them off slowly as the price goes in your favor? Should you wait for a specific price target before you close it? And what if the trade starts going against you? When should you get out?

By now I'm sure you've noticed a pattern in this book: there are SO many different ways to do literally *everything* as you trade, and managing the trade is no different. I am a professional, and even I will open & close many trades that make me think, *"I could have done that a little better."* Sometimes I've paid myself before the trade had a chance to *really* work, so in hindsight I see that I would have made more if I had stayed in longer. Other times I've closed out too quickly when the trade started to go against me. If I had stayed in I would have made money instead of lost money once the price reversed in my favor. And sometimes I've lost money because I stayed in *way* too long... I should have closed out earlier and minimized my losses.

Occasionally I'll have a 'nearly perfect' trade, which means entry and exit very close to the absolute peak & valley of the movement, therefore maximizing my profit. Honestly, this is rare. I have good trades every single day, but I don't normally have *perfect* trades. The good news is, you don't *need* to have perfect trades to make great money doing this. You only need to be *in the ballpark* consistently. If you opened a trade at $200 per contract and then closed it at $250 per contract, so what if it eventually went to $280 per contract?

For the example above—obviously in hindsight it would have been better to ride it out longer—but **YOU STILL MADE MONEY.** Whether you make $100 per day or $1,000 per day, that money is money you were able to make in your bathrobe with a few mouse clicks. Where else can you do that? Nowhere. Any other endeavor that can make you this much money this easily is illegal.

PREMIUM PRICING

It's important to understand one of the major differences between trading OPTIONS and simply buying and selling stock: with stocks, you only need to worry about ONE number—the price of that stock. If you buy stock you just wait for the price to go up to sell at a later date, and if the price goes down you sell when it's too painful for you to hold on any longer. But with options contracts, you need to worry about many more things—including the passage of time which de-values your contracts as time passes *(Theta decay)* and the options premium on the contract(s), which can change rapidly depending on a number of different factors.

For example, if you buy an options contract that expires in one month, the passage of one day will have no noticeable affect on the price of your contract. Of course, the price of your contract will go up or down depending on what happened in the markets that day, but the passage of one day's worth of time alone won't make a noticeable difference in the price of that contract.

But if you bought an options contract that expires that *same day*, then time decay will greatly affect the price of your contract, as each passing minute represents a much greater totality of the time left until expiration. So even if price moved completely sideways throughout the day, your contract would be drastically less valuable at 3PM than it was at 9AM, simply because there's virtually no time left until expiration. You can think about this in human terms: for a 10 year old, one year represents 10% of their entire life. For a 100 year old person, that same one year represents just 1% of their entire life. The more time you have left until expiration, the less significant each day is in relation to time value.

Right now you might be asking yourself, *"Why not just buy stock if it's so much easier?"* The answer is: LEVERAGE. One options contract typically represents control over 100 shares of the underlying stock. And since one options contract lets you control a larger position in the underlying asset for a fraction of the cost compared to buying the stock outright, that leverage can amplify profits if the trade goes in your favor. But remember—this also means options can be a lot more dangerous if you don't know what you're doing... so that's why it's so important to study up and gain confidence *before* getting into any real size with your trading.

If you were trying to *invest* money in a company you believed would grow over time, then simply buying stock in that company could be a good idea. But that's not what this book is about. Day trading is NOT investing. Investing is *parking* money. Day trading is *moving* money each day.

The sooner you can get your head wrapped around how options premium works, the better off you'll be. Options premium *(often referred to simply as premium),* is the price that a buyer pays to purchase an options contract from a seller. It represents the cost or price of the option itself and is one of the fundamental aspects of options trading. The premium is determined by various factors and can vary from one option to another.

Options premium is composed of two main components:

1. Intrinsic Value: This is the portion of the premium that represents the real or inherent value of the option. Your options contract is 'in the money' (ITM) if the contract you hold is currently worth more than the underlying asset. For example, a $2.65 call option is ITM if the underlying asset is currently trading for $2.80 *(you could buy shares of the underlying stock for $2.65 per share, while someone without the option will have to pay $2.80 for the same share)*. Conversely, a $2.80 put option would be ITM if the underlying asset was currently trading for $2.65.

2. Time Value: Time value represents the portion of the premium that is not attributed to intrinsic value. It accounts for factors such as the time remaining until the option's expiration, expected future price movements, implied volatility, and interest rates. Time value diminishes as the option approaches its expiration date. Therefore, if you're trading weekly expirations, a contract you purchase on Monday with a Friday expiration will have *more* time value than that same contract purchased on Wednesday. As time passes, your time value diminishes.

Several factors impact the premium of an options contract, including:

- Underlying Asset Price: As the price of the underlying asset moves, the premium of the associated options can change.

- Strike Price: The relationship between the strike price and the current market price of the underlying asset affects the premium. In-the-money options have higher premiums.

- Time to Expiration: Options with more time until expiration typically have higher premiums because they have more time for the underlying asset's price to move in a favorable direction.

- Volatility: Increased implied volatility often leads to higher premiums because it suggests a greater potential for price movements.

- Bid and Ask Prices: The premium of an options contract is typically quoted as a bid price and an ask price. The bid price represents the maximum price a buyer is willing to pay, while the ask price represents the minimum price a seller is willing to accept.

And now that we've covered the basics of what options premium is, let's talk more about one of the most important factors mentioned above as it relates to my style of trading:

VOLATILITY. Once you understand how volatility affects options premium, you'll immediately realize why trading first thing in the morning is the best time to do it.

I'm not telling you to hit the 'buy' button in the first minute of the market open every day, and I'm not saying you can't make good money trading later on during the day—but if you *are* able to trade right at the open and and you want to take advantage of bigger swings in options premium due to the increased volatility that occurs in the morning, you should try to be in a position no later than 15-20 minutes into the morning session *(at the first sign of a valid entry point).*

So how does volatility play a significant role in determining options premium? Here are a few reasons:

- Increased Volatility Increases Premium: When the market experiences higher volatility, the premium of options tends to rise. This is because greater volatility implies a higher likelihood of significant price swings or larger price movements in the underlying asset. Traders are willing to pay more for options that have the potential for substantial gains.

- Time Value Component: Volatility is a critical component of an option's time value. Options have two main components to their premium: intrinsic value *(the difference between the option's strike price and the underlying asset's current price)* and time value.

Higher volatility increases the time value portion of the premium because it implies a greater likelihood of the option becoming profitable before expiration.

- Implied Volatility Impact: Implied volatility (IV) specifically measures the market's expectations for future volatility. When IV is elevated *(like at the beginning of the day)*, options premiums rise in anticipation of larger price fluctuations.

- Risk and Reward Considerations: While higher volatility can lead to higher premiums, it also increases the potential for larger price swings, which can be both an opportunity and a risk for day traders. You should carefully assess the relationship between options premiums, volatility, and the overall risk-reward profile before you make a trade.

There were many times when I was first starting out *(I had a small account)* and I wanted to make a trade, but the options premiums were just too high for me. I didn't want to risk such a large chunk of my capital on just a few contracts. This is something you'll need to consider, depending on the size of your capital. If you're working with a $50,000 account, then this will never be an issue. But if you have $1,000-$5,000, then the price of each individual contract can become more consequential.

For example: let's say you have $1,000 of capital to work with. You might look at an at-the-money META option that costs $450 per contract, or a next day's expiration at-the-money QQQ option which costs $150 per contract... even though the same sized move on the META option would make you more money *per contract* vs. QQQ due to the higher price, with 1K you would only be able to afford 2 META contracts. But you would be able to afford 6 of the QQQ contracts for about the same price.

I would rather have 6 contacts to work with than 2. The more contracts you hold, the more latitude you have in your entries and exits. Using the above example, if you are trading META, you've got just 2 'ins and outs' versus 6 ins and outs with the QQQ's. And the more flexibility you'll have in your entries & exits, the better your chances will be. You have to be more 'perfect' with your entries and exits when you have less contracts.

Think about it: if you have ONE contract, that's it. You've got ONE shot to get it right. But if you hold 100 contracts of that same option, you could be 'pretty good' with 50 of them, 'great' with 30 of them, and you could completely shit the bed with the last 20, and you *still* would have made money. The old adage 'it takes money to make money' is very applicable here. The more money you have to work with, the less perfect you need to be in order to make money.

TIME CONSIDERATIONS

Now I'm going to discuss a few more ways that the passage of time can affect your trades. As with everything else in life, hindsight is always 20/20. If you see the price of a stock steadily rise all week long, and you made money a few days of the week going long but didn't hold any positions open overnight, it might be tempting to think, *"I should have just held the position open all week and made even more as a swing trade."* Sure, this reality is possible in many situations, but remember—*hindsight* is 20/20. Foresight is NOT.

Just because in hindsight you realize that holding an option open *would have* made you more money, that's no reason to do it. Why? Because with the passage of time comes increased risk and unpredictability. As I've tried to hammer home in this book so far—in the trading game, risk and unpredictability are your worst enemies.

One thing that I love about day trading is that by getting in and out of the position in the same day, we eliminate all of the unknowns that might happen while we're sleeping. For example: Overnight, one country may decide to declare war against another. The CEO of the company you have an open position on gets busted for some nefarious activity. The US credit rating gets downgraded. All of these aforementioned things have *actually happened* in real life, and the list goes on and on. The market often reacts to the 'unforeseen circumstances' that occur after-hours by creating gaps.

GAPS

I introduced you to gaps back in chapter 5, but here's a visual so you can see what it actually looks like on a chart, and what it can mean for your trading.

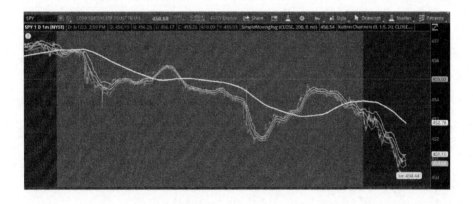

Above we see an example of an overnight gap down on SPY. The black areas on the left and right side of the chart represent the end and beginning of market hours, and the grey space in the middle represents the overnight hours. You can see from the number on the right side of the image that SPY closed at approximately 456.5, and then opened at approximately 453.3. This means that overnight SPY gapped DOWN over 3 points, which is NOT an insignificant number *(anything more than 1 point is a decent move).*

The most important takeaway you can make from all of this info is: **GAPS INTRODUCE UNPREDICTABILITY INTO YOUR TRADES.** Yeah, I've made money on large overnight gaps, but I've also lost money on them. The point is—when you are right there, present and focused on your trades from open to close, then YOU are the only one who controls your fate.

In a perfect world we would never deal with gaps because we would never hold overnight. That's a rule I have made for myself: **NEVER HOLD OVERNIGHT.** Of course, sometimes I *do* hold overnight, but that's a rare occurrence. I won't get into the specific circumstances that need to occur in order for me hold overnight, because I don't want YOU to hold overnight. Just don't do it. It's never fun to wake up and feel like you're about to spin a roulette wheel to find out whether price gapped up or down, for or against you.

FIXING YOUR AVERAGE PRICE

Many times I'll open a trade and add to that position before I close it, whether I'm winning *or* losing. I realize this might sound confusing. You may be thinking to yourself, *"If you're winning why not just sell for a profit, and if you're losing why not just stop out and minimize your losses?"* Sometimes I *do* react this way when either one of those scenarios plays out, but other times I'll add to the position before I close it out. What is the difference maker that determines whether I just close the position or add to it? That all depends on how much *confidence* I have that my initial idea was correct.

When you decide to enter a trade, one of two things will happen:

1. You buy an initial amount of options contracts, then sell those contracts when it's the right time to close your position *(ideally for a large profit)*.
2. You buy an initial amount of options contracts and then add more contracts to that initial position before you close the position.

Right now, we're only talking about option 2, because this is the way to 'fix' your average price. What does that mean? It's what happens when you have conviction in a trade idea but the trade doesn't go your way immediately, *or* when the trade *is* going your way and you want to add in on slight pullbacks, for even bigger profits.

For example: Let's say during premarket you notice some information on the daily chart telling you today *should* shape up to be a bullish day, and you're pretty confident of that based on what you see. When the market opens up you buy 3 call options for $100 a piece about 10 minutes into the session, when you see the right time to enter based on the 1 minute chart. But right after you open your position, price drops for a few consecutive candles. At this point, there are three things you could do:

1. Close the position for a loss *(not recommended in most cases)*

2. Hold steady for a while longer, waiting to see what happens

3. Add to your position *(fixing your average price)*

Number three is a good option IF you're very confident that the present move against you is just a slight hiccup and not a reversing trend. The *less* confident you are in what you're seeing on the chart, the less you should add in *(if you add in at all)*. Remember: only add in when you have a LOT of confidence that your original idea was correct. Because if you're wrong about this, you'll lose even more money than you were already losing before you added-in, and nobody wants that.

But when you ARE confident that your original idea was correct, then adding in when it dips against you can be a great idea, because if & when the stock does move in your favor, then you'll make even more money than you would have with your initial investment.

Here's an example:

Let's say you bought 3 call options on AMD for $100 each. Right after you buy it the price dips, and suddenly each contract is only worth $90. If you close now you'll lose $30, plus commissions. But if you ADD IN and buy three *more* contracts here, your average price is lowered. You've got your $300 initial investment plus $270 when the price is at $90 *($90 x 3)*, so 300+270=$570. 570 divided by 6 equals 95. So now in total, each one of your contracts actually cost you $95 a piece rather than $100 a piece. This is an extremely simplistic example that would never play out exactly like this in real life *(with all the whole numbers)*, I just wanted to give you a very easy to understand scenario.

Adding in is something I do frequently, and it works a lot more often than it doesn't. You just need to be conscious of monitoring your cash levels *(make sure you've got some 'bullets in the chamber')*. Even though you'll make more profits by playing with bigger size, I don't like using all of my available capital each day.

As a general rule, it's a good idea to keep a large chunk of your available capital as a reserve, just in case you have a really bad day... the LAST thing you want to do is blow up your account, which can happen if you go too big and then mismanage the trade. But don't worry—you won't do that as long as you pay attention to everything I'm saying. Nobody else can *make you* blow up your account. If you *do* blow up, there's no one to blame but yourself. So DO NOT be that person.

You don't need to be losing in order to benefit from adding in after your initial buy. Here's an example of how adding in can help you profit, even after your average price is *raised.*

Let's go back to our previous example. You buy 3 call options on AMD at $100 a piece. But this time, your initial idea was correct and you're immediately green on the trade. Before you know it, your contracts are each worth $110. You could close out the position here for a profit of $30, but if you're confident that the trend is strong and price will continue to rise, you can wait until a small pullback happens and then *add* to your position *(this is called 'buying the dip')*.

So, if price is at $110 per contract and you see a quick dip in price to $105 per contract, you can add in here and buy 3 more contracts. Your average price will be *higher* now, because you bought 3 contracts at $100 a piece and then three more at $105 dollars a piece... but now you have *six* contracts instead of *three*, and more size equals more profit when things are going your way. So if price suddenly pops back up and goes back to $110 or higher, you're making more profit even though your average price has gone up. Being able to sell SIX contracts for $110 a piece that each cost you $102.50 is better than being able to sell THREE contracts for $110 a piece that each cost you $100.

REMEMBER: the key to adding in *(whether you're winning or losing)* is being *confident* that price action will go where you think it will go. NO confidence = NO add-in. Also remember, more size = more gains OR losses, always. So be sure to keep that in mind whenever you're considering what size to trade with. This is why I always suggest trading ONE contract per day until you become very comfortable with everything about the process.

AVOID DISTRACTIONS

It's pretty cool that you can watch CNBC on TOS by adding a little gadget on the left hand side—but avoid doing this while you have open trades. It's amazing how easy it is to get distracted, and divided attention is never as good as paying full attention to your trades. I always trade with complete silence and 100% focus.

Remember back in chapter 3 when I talked about the importance of having a dedicated office? Once you're doing this for real, you'll quickly realize just how important it is. Being able to shut the door and shut out all distractions is essential. I believe that multi-tasking is highly overrated. I'd much rather focus on doing *one thing* at a time, and doing that one thing well. The more privacy you have, and the less distractions you have, the more successful you'll be. It's that simple.

OK, now that you've opened a position… whether you have 1 contract or 100 contracts, the MOST important thing to remember when you are *in* the trade is:

DON'T GET SCARED, AND DON'T GET GREEDY

Desire and fear, the only true motivators in life. You will feel both of these emotions while you are in a trade. Don't give in to either one of them. Trade the chart, not your emotions. Always. And in practical terms this means: don't stop out too early, and don't hold on too long. There's a perfect time to enter and a perfect time to exit, and it's your job to get as close as possible to perfection with both.

If you let fear guide your actions, you'll either wait too long before you enter, looking for *too much* confirmation and therefore missing out on the ideal entry price, or else you'll get out too early, because you got over excited at your 5% gain… when you should have waited another 20 minutes to see that 5% become 15%.

If you let greed guide your actions, you might hold on *too* long… trying to get 'just a little more…' and then 'just a *little* bit more'… and before you know it you're Icarus, watching your profits melt before your eyes, when you should have closed out a few minutes earlier and walked away with very respectable gains.

Once you get to the point where you avoid making decisions based on fear or greed, you're on your way to long-term success. In the next chapter I'll get into what to look for on the charts while you're in the trade… and even more importantly, *how* to look at the charts.

CHAPTER 11

The Art of the Chart

"Everything you can imagine is real." — Pablo Picasso

One of the most surprising things I discovered at the beginning of my trading journey is this: before I knew anything about the stock market, I thought a person needed to be good at NUMBERS and STATISTICS in order to be a successful trader, and that's one of the reasons I *almost* didn't even try. But the reality is, this couldn't be farther from the truth.

I've never been a numbers person, and I was always terrible at math in school. I'm your quintessential left-handed, right-brained person. I'm all about creativity, and music, and writing, and art. And guess what? Being an artistic person is one of the best traits a trader can have. More specifically— **being able to see the charts as art.**

What does this mean? All of these little candlesticks flickering up and down are not random. Yes, there are 'chance events' that happen in the market, but chance events happen everywhere, every day. Just because a thing *could* happen doesn't mean that it probably *will* happen. I mean, you could get struck by lighting or win the lottery tomorrow *(or even both on the same day)...* but what are the *realistic* chances of that actually happening?

This is why, when you're able to view the candlesticks on the chart as a type of visual artwork, you can see the patterns emerging before your eyes... patterns that are far from random.

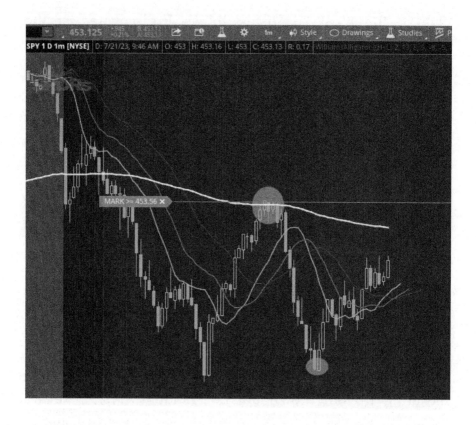

In the example above, we see how we could have made money both ways *(long or short)* simply by recognizing the strength of the pattern developing right before our eyes.

There are actually 3 places I would feel comfortable trading on this chart, 2 short and one long. The first would be to get in short right around where the word 'MARK' is. The Alligator is trending noticeably bearish, and as soon as price rejects the bottom line of the Alligator and then breaks below the 200 EMA, I'm comfortable going short there. You could have spent 15-20 minutes making profits until the huge green engulfing candle at the bottom left point of the 'W' forced you to stop out the rest.

The second place I'd be comfortable going short is at the middle highlighted oval section when price rides the 200 EMA for a few minutes and then rejects. You could have made an additional 8-10 minutes of profits here before price once again reverses at the bottom right tip of the 'W.' And this is where it would be OK to flip to a long bias, since the next 2 green candles after the engulfing candle have established this as a true double bottom. As you can see, there's at least 15 minutes of profits to be made going long from here.

I should note that from these 3 possible trades, I would have the MOST confidence in the first one, when price first broke below the 200 EMA at the 12-15 minute mark. I would have less confidence in the second short trade, when price bounces off the 200 EMA, and I would have the least amount of confidence in the third trade, going long.

Why the least amount of confidence with the long trade? Simply because the 200 EMA is still trending down and price is still sitting below it. That's not to say I wouldn't take the long trade here—I would. I just wouldn't trade with as much size as I'd be comfortable using in the first or second trade. The point is: you can make money going both directions, sometimes even long AND short within 30 minutes.

Everyone's seen cop shows where the detective has the big cork board on the wall, filled with photos of potential suspects, press clippings about the crime, pieces of string connecting multiple elements. Theres always that ubiquitous scene of the detective giving the board a hard, steely-eyed stare just before the proverbial 'lightbulb' goes off in their head and they crack the case. This is not so different than what we see when we study charts.

The importance of interpreting the meaning of price action using different time frames, levels and indicators cannot be overstated. A pattern or level will seem to have meaning when viewed in one time frame, but maybe not in another. It's your job to be a detective and assign more significance to certain pieces of information and less to others, in order to see 'the big picture'.

This is why I'm always stressing the importance of GETTING CONFIRMATION before making any moves. Just like cops shouldn't arrest someone based on one piece of flimsy evidence, you shouldn't enter or exit a trade because you saw ONE thing that gave you that idea. Of course, we will see things all day every day that give us ideas... the point is, with the proper confirmation you can determine which signals are 'real' and which signals are fake outs.

We've already covered the most important candlestick patterns like the double top, double bottom, flags, head and shoulders, dojis, engulfing, etc. I won't repeat all of that info here. But it's important to realize that everything on the screen is connected. Seeing valid patters and trends and then acting on these things is the 'bread and butter' of this strategy. You can be affected by things beyond your control, but you must act when you see a setup that you have strong confidence in *(based on your technical analysis and confirmation)*.

FACING THE INEVITABLE

Speaking of being affected by things beyond your control, I need to warm you: there WILL be times when a certain piece of financial information or news is released, and that information might tank your position, even when you did everything correctly. This just goes to show—you can do everything right and still lose money. Of course, that's no reason to *not* trade, just be aware... these sorts of things WILL happen to you.

It's important for your own confidence and development to be able to tell the difference between losses due to your own mistakes and losses due to factors beyond your control. It's OK to beat yourself up a bit when YOU messed up. Figure out what you did wrong and figure out how to NOT do those same things again. But don't beat yourself up about things beyond your control. Just dust yourself off, trust the process and do it all again the next day.

SEE THE CHART AS ART. The importance of this cannot be underestimated. The charts are art, they are not just data. If you can SEE the charts as art, then you can recognize the patterns that give you clues as to where price action will head next.

CHAPTER 12

Exits

"Have I played the part well? Then applaud as I exit."

—Augustus

I tend to get out of a trade fairly quickly after I enter it. I don't usually scalp *(which sometimes takes only minutes between opening and closing)*, but I do try to keep a roughly 30-minute to one hour limit on the amount of time I spend between the opening and closing of all contracts for that trade. Enough time to let the trend work, but not enough time for the trend to run out of steam and reverse on me.

When you're considering the 'best' time to exit a day trade, think about the concept of time itself. I briefly touched on this idea earlier in the book, but I'll expand on it a bit here. Take a moment to think about how you feel right NOW. Do you feel great? Do you feel like shit? Perhaps somewhere in-between? Whatever the answer is, identify these specific feelings.

If I asked you, *"How certain are you that you know exactly how you'll feel 5 minutes from now?"* Your answer would probably be, *"I'm 99% sure I can tell you exactly how I'll feel 5 minutes from now."*

If I asked you the same question, except this time I've changed the time frame from 5 minutes to 5 hours, your confidence level will go down. You'd still feel pretty confident you can predict how you'll feel in 5 hours, but certainly with less confidence than 5 minutes from now. And finally, if I asked again except this time I changed the time frame to 5 weeks from now, your confidence level would plummet.

I'm nearly 100% certain I know how I'll feel 5 minutes from now. But 5 weeks? Who knows? A million things could happen between now and 5 weeks from now. The same concept applies to day trading. You can feel the most confident working with time frames that are the closest to right NOW.

This is why I day trade, and why I always prefer to open and close trades in as short a time frame as possible, while obviously maximizing profits. Sometimes it's better to stay in a position for a few hours rather than 30 minutes... but each situation is different, so always trade the charts and trade based on what you see right in front of your eyes rather than a preconceived notion of what your exact timing 'should' be.

If you've only been in the position for 10 minutes but it looks like the trend has suddenly run out of steam, then it's time to get out. But if you've been in the trade for 90 minutes and it's still going strong, don't close your position just because you think, *"I've been in over an hour, this is too long..."* just let the momentum keep working for as long as it wants to. Let the chart tell you when to get out. Remember, each situation is different, and although we need to have rough guidelines to follow, nothing is set in stone. **Always trade based on what you see right in front of your eyes.**

KNOWING WHEN TO LEAVE THE PARTY

Knowing exactly when and how to exit your position requires more nuance and skill than perhaps any other aspect of trading. *Before* you enter a position, everything is theoretical. *After* you exit your position, everything is final and there's nothing left to chance or worry about. But each second you're *in the trade*, your entire position is in flux.

This is why setting price targets AND stop loss levels is important. Have a plan for how much you want to make *and* how much you'll accept to lose, *before* you open a position. When you enter a trade, you can never be sure whether it will go for or against you, so you need to have a plan and be prepared for either outcome.

That specific number *(the gains you desire or losses you'll accept)* will be different for everyone, and that's a personal style you'll need to develop over time as you trade. If you wanted to make your profit and stop-loss targets extremely cut and dried, you could just say, *"I'm closing my position when I gain 15% or lose 5% today, whichever happens first."* That's not how I trade nor would I encourage you to, but you *could* do that if you wanted to.

Let's say you have 10 open contracts and price is moving in your favor, albeit slowly. Now you're posed with a question: should you sell all of your contracts at once when price reaches a certain level, or have a few different price targets set and sell some at one level and the rest at a second level, or just 'feel the chart' and continuously sell contracts as price moves in your favor?

Normally I prefer the third option, for a few reasons. For one thing, just like how adding in can 'fix' your average price, slowly easing out of the position can average out your gains while simultaneously locking in profits and reducing risk. With each contract sold, you eliminate risk because you only have risk on open contracts. Any contracts that are closed are off the table—no more profits *or* losses are possible on a contract once it's closed.

My preferred method of trading is to watch the chart closely, and scale out of trades on big pushes when price is going in my favor. So, if I'm long I'll exit on big green candles. If I'm short I'll exit on big red candles. I'll scale the amount and size of my exits based on how much strength I see in the trend. If a trend looks VERY strong and I think there's a large chance it continues for hours, I'll tend to be a bit riskier by leaving more positions open in an attempt to catch a larger chunk of the total move. If I feel like the trend is weak, or if I see that it's becoming exhausted, I'll be quicker to get out and pull profits before the trend reverses on me.

Below is an example of a long trade I had on Meta, from entry to exit.

As you can see in the first highlighted oval where it says 'enter here'—this is where I opened my position with 5 contracts. Why did I open here? For multiple reasons. First, the 50 EMA has gained a bit of distance above the 200 EMA here. I could have opened about 5 minutes earlier when price, Alligator, 50 and 200 EMA were all converging at the same point, but there wasn't enough long-bias confirmation for me at that point.

It would have been easy for price to break lower since all of it was converging at one spot. But 5 minutes later on, it had established it's bullish trend by creating a higher high and a higher low. I got in right at the small green candle right after the small red candle *(inside the highlighted oval)*. And you can see, right after that there was a bigger green candle, and it shot up from there for about the next 10 minutes.

I took my first profits at the far left 'take profit' oval. When it plateaued, I wanted to lock in some profits just in case it decided to wash out suddenly. I thought it had more steam to move higher *(which it did)*, but I wanted to give myself some insurance just in case—remember, once you sell one or more contracts, you're then 'locked in' to whatever price you received for those contracts. At that point, your P&L for the contracts you just closed is *actual* and not *theoretical*. I closed 2 contracts at this point, leaving me with 3 open and 2 closed for a profit.

Price then flagged back to the bottom of the Alligator, and I added in here, with an additional 3 contracts. This looks scary, right? Three fairly large red candles in a row. So why did I ADD here instead of closing the rest of my positions to protect my profits?

A few reasons. First, price was still above the 50 EMA, and at this point the 50 EMA was well above the 200 EMA. Those 2 EMA's had grown much further apart than they were just 10 minutes earlier. So those are all very bullish signals. Second, price never broke below the jaw of the Alligator, so that told me any bearish pressure was just a flag and not a legit trend reversal. Once I saw that large engulfing green candle to the right of the small red candle inside the oval, that's when I jumped in again. And that move paid off, with another big push up for the next 10 minutes.

At this point I had 6 open contracts. As the price plateaued at the top of the image *(at the 2nd "take profit" oval)*, that's what I started to think the trend was getting exhausted. For that 10 minute consolidation period, I closed out a few more contracts, one-by-one on the pushes up. This is yet another example of why the 1-minute chart is the ONLY chart we look at when entering *or* exiting.

If you're in long and you've decided it's time to exit, you always want to make that exit as close as possible to the 'top-tick' of the 1-minute candle *(if the candle has a wick, this would mean exiting when price was at the absolute top of the wick on a green candle.)* If you're in short, it's the same thing but in reverse, so you'd be looking to exit at the absolute bottom of the wick of a red candle.

After closing most of my contracts in this highlighted plateau period, I left one contract open. Why just one contract? Because I thought there was a possibility for another push higher, but I also knew it could easily break down since at this point there was no more sustained pressure to the upside... we were consolidating here. I didn't have a lot of confidence in either direction, so therefore I held just one contract open. This was so I could make a bit more if price *did* have enough juice for one more push, but I wouldn't lose much if price washed out.

As you can see, it turns out price *did* indeed wash out a few minutes later. I held my last contract open until price broke below the 50 EMA, because at that point I knew the trend had reversed and we were now in for a bearish ride. Price flagged for a few minutes about 10 minutes after that, but then washed out HARD.

Notice the head and shoulders pattern that develops here, which is a bearish pattern. It's pretty easy to spot the left shoulder, head, and right shoulder *(which is thinner than the left)*. This pattern vaguely resembles a silhouette of a person's upper torso, hence the name "head and shoulders."Most patterns won't look like a perfect representation of what they're supposed to be *(this head & shoulders doesn't look exactly like a person's torso)*... but you get the point. A double bottom will closely resemble the letter W just like a double top will closely resemble the letter M. If you can spot these patterns as they develop, you're on your way to continued success.

In hindsight you can see that I would have made even more money by simply going short at the right shoulder. Had I done that, the ride down from the right shoulder all the way to the bottom of the image would have made me a LOT more money than the long trade I did take at the left side of the image. But that's OK! I still made money going long with the trade that I *did* take, so I was happy.

The point is: there's always a way to make money, short or long—all day long. Patterns like this develop constantly. Although I prefer to trade first thing in the morning, you can trade at any time of the day and spot opportunities like this. Price action won't normally be as dramatic later on in the day *(which means less volatility, and that's bad for me)* but the point is you *can* find opportunities at any time. Don't avoid trading all together just because you can't trade the first hour of the day.

So back to the trade I *did* take. You can see how easy it is to predict price action when you have multiple pieces of information all giving you confirmation. Upon my entry, price had just made higher highs AND higher low, price was sitting at the top of the Alligator indicator, which was itself over the 50 EMA. And the 50 EMA had recently crossed over the 200 EMA. All of these things are very bullish signals.

Here are the 4 different signals that told me the trend was bullish:

1. Higher highs + higher lows

2. Alligator trending upwards, with price in top half of the indicator

3. Alligator stacked above 50 EMA

4. 50 EMA stacked above 200 EMA

When you start being able to see and interpret multiple pieces of information at once, that's when the magic happens. At first, you'll find yourself focusing on one thing at a time, but the more experience you gain, the more you'll be able to see a lot of things happening simultaneously. Remember: price can change QUICKLY... one minute you have $200 of profit, and 5 minutes later you might have $50. This is the main reason we always watch the 1 minute chart when considering entries and exits. You need the most immediate price action available.

SEEING THE FOREST THROUGH THE TREES

This next section will provide an example of 2 important things: why having the right indicators and the right *amount* of indicators is so important, and why it's so essential to combine the visual information you get from ALL of your indicators into one 'bigger picture' view. The very heart of successful trading is essentially having the ability to predict the future based on what we see on the charts. Therefore, you need to take the individual pieces of information on your charts and indicators, then combine them and see them as a unified whole. See the *whole chart,* not just the disconnected elements of the chart. I'll now explain how being able to connect multiple pieces of information from your charts and indicators can give you a much better holistic view of price action.

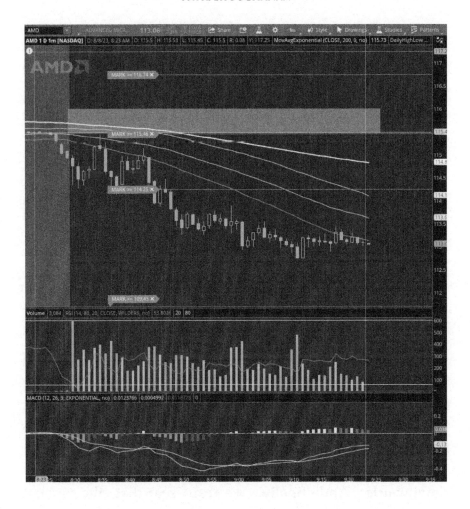

This 1 minute AMD chart above shows us a weakening bearish trend. The price action is still trending negative, but the *strength* of the negative trend is weakening, meaning- if you're already in short and you're working the trade, it might be a good time to think about your exit.

As you look at the screenshot of the chart, don't just focus on each individual indicator—combine everything you see in the image to get the bigger picture. If you were to only look at ONE indicator, you would get one idea that may conflict with the information you'd get if you looked at a different indicator by itself. Here's what I mean.

In the image above, if we ONLY look at the candlesticks, we see that price action is steadily falling. Looks fully bearish, right? Yes, BUT... when we look at the MACD over the same timeframe, we can see the strength increasing, with green bars appearing over the zero line, and the 12 EMA crossing over the 26 EMA, and we see the directional slant of the EMA lines moving upward. These are all bullish signals. And then when we look at the RSI *(which is overlapped onto the volume chart)* we can see that the overall strength trend is climbing.

Next, when we look at the volume, we can see that those 2 large red bars in the middle didn't really move the price downwards. And finally, we can see that the spatial relationship of the candlesticks to the Keltner Channels is tightening. Right around the 8:45-8:50AM time frame there's a good bit of distance between the candlesticks sitting lower than the bottom line of the Keltner Channels. But by 9:20-9:25AM, the candles are actually touching the bottom line of the channel. The closer proximity of the candles to the

Keltner Channels also indicates a reversal may be happening soon.

So, all of this sets up what is called a 'divergence'—which means a certain piece of information is telling you one thing, but another piece of information tells you something different. In this case, the price action is showing us downward movement, but everything else is giving us bullish signals.

Now don't be mistaken—this is NOT a sign to go long here. I would need MUCH more confirmation that a bullish trend is actually setting up before I would get long. But if I were *already* in a short position at this moment, I'd be paying very close attention and thinking about my exit, especially if price breaks above the top of the green candle 6 minutes to the left of the far right candle.

I wouldn't say this chart is especially *dangerous* to a short... because there's a good possibility that the price action will simply consolidate for a while and then fall again, so I wouldn't be in a rush to get out right away, but all of this chart information would make me be hyper-focused on what happens during the next 5-10 minutes.

To sum up the 'correct' way to think about your exits:

- **Let the chart tell you when it's time to exit** (*don't trade based on a rigid timeframe*)

- **Don't let fear or greed keep you from making the right decisions**

- **Always get confirmation from multiple sources before you exit**

- **Have defined profit and stop loss targets set, and follow them**

- **Develop your own style of profit and loss acceptance** *(there's no 'one size fits all' way to do it)*

And since this is the chapter about EXITS, I should mention the exit *after* the exit. What I mean is—once you're finished with your trades, walk away from the computer and go do something else. You got into this to give yourself more free time right? If so, then don't let *this* job become a replacement for your *last* job. There's no reason to watch every second of market action unfold once you've closed *your* trades.

You're NOT chained to your desk from 9-5. No fake smiles are needed here. No 'firm handshakes' or unbroken eye contact required. There's no Bill Lumbergh lurking over your shoulder, and you don't need to put the new coversheet on your TPS report. You are the master of your own destiny now. And so I implore you—when you're finished trading, just walk away and enjoy your life. The market will still be here tomorrow.

Chapter 13

The Game of Risk

"Better to die on one's feet than to live on one's knees."

—Jean Paul Sartre

OK, I have good news and bad news regarding RISK in the stock market.

Here's the bad news: Managing risk is one of the most unscientific, fluid, nuanced aspects of trading. There is no bulletproof, 'one size fits all' approach to risk. It's always situational, and even when you make the same move multiple times, that move won't always result in the same outcome each time. It's frustrating, I know. Ultimately, only YOU can decide how much risk you are willing to deal with, and then accept the consequences of that decision.

If you took 10 skilled traders and showed each of them a well defined double-top or double-bottom pattern, they would all see the same thing. But take those same 10 traders and ask each one of them to describe what 'acceptable risk' is, and you'll probably get 10 different answers. There are a lot of ways you can manage your risk, and all of them could be ideal in certain situations- but none of them will be perfect in *every* situation.

But here's the good news: the level of risk you accept is one of the few things *you have absolute control* over in the world of day trading. Nobody else can make you risk more than you're willing to risk. Nobody else can *make you* play with 80% of your account if you're only comfortable playing with 20% of it. Nobody else can *make you* stay in a trade after you've decided it's time to stop out.

If a trade goes against you and you decide to set a hard stop at -5% *(meaning you close the position after you've lost 5% on the trade)*, then you'll do that and know you won't lose more than 5% on that trade. Even though we can never guarantee what the market will do, we *can* guarantee how much risk we're willing to accept. Obviously, the less risk you accept the less you stand to lose. But remember, risk is also tied to your ability to make profit. Less risk=less potential profits OR losses, and vice-versa.

The 'woulda, coulda, shoulda' feeling is something you'd better get used to... because you WILL have that feeling often. There are SO many times I've thought to myself, *"I should have stayed in longer"* or, *"I should have stopped out sooner"*... get used to the sound of your own voice telling you these things. But ultimately that's OK, because even when we don't capture 100% of the move, we're still winning 70-80% of the time, and that's a perfectly acceptable number.

So *how* exactly do we mitigate risk, you ask? Here are a few ways:

Some people go for the ultra-conservative approach, so they'll set a stop order the second they open a trade. What that means is— they have a predetermined amount they're willing to lose before they close the trade. That stop order can be set for an exact price target or a percentage.

For example, if you set a stop order to close your position at -5%, then the second you've LOST 5% on your trade, your trading software will automatically place a closing trade for you. You're out of the position, and now you will not lose any more money than you've already lost on the day... but if the stock suddenly reverses and goes in your favor a minute *after* you close that position, you will not get any of your losses back. The moment you close your position, you will not have any more profits *or* losses on that position.

Another thing you can do is set a trailing stop order, which means that if you're winning and think you might be able to squeeze some more profits out of a move, the stop will move along with the price action. For example: you buy a call option contract for $100 and immediately set a trailing stop order for -10%. This means that if the price suddenly drops below $90 for that contract, your trading software will automatically close the position. But if the price climbs and climbs all day, that -10% trailing stop order will move with it... so if by the end of the day your $100 contract is trading for $150, your brokerage will now sell if the price drops below $135, not $90 (*-10% from $150*).

Trailing stops can be used very effectively, but just like everything in trading there's an art to it. When I set a trailing stop I like to use that day's largest candle size to visualize what the exact stop will be. And how I do that is: I see how big the biggest negative candles are for that day (*or recent days if I'm doing this first thing in the morning*).

The reason for this is: the stock will show us what it's range is like, and I can react to what it's telling me rather than just assigning a random number. So, if the biggest swings on the day represent a 12% move, I probably don't want to set my trailing stop at 10%, because it could easily surpass my stop by *just this much* and then reverse back in my favor as soon as my software has stopped me out. Obviously I don't want that.

I can tell you from personal experience, there are few things more frustrating than getting stopped out because of a trailing stop order, only to watch the price reverse and rip for the rest of the day in the direction I wanted it to go in the first place. The BEST case scenario is to simply be in front of your screens for the entirety of the trade, so you can know exactly when you want to exit. But sometimes the unexpected happens, and in these moments you'll need to choose whether to refrain from trading entirely that day, or set a stop/trailing stop order after you open the trade.

CRUNCHING THE NUMBERS

Another thing that weighs heavily on risk is the size of your trading account. In a perfect world, it would be great to never have to risk more than 10% of your account on any given day. This is one of many instances where the old analogy 'it takes money to make money' comes into play. It's pretty easy to follow the 10% rule AND make substantial money if you have $20,000 in your account. That means you could risk $2,000 on trades every day *(10% of your account)*—and if you trade smart, playing with 2k is more than enough to make at least $300-$500 per day without getting too risky with your time involvement *(more on what I mean by 'time involvement' in a minute)*.

If you have a total of $2,000 in your trading account rather than $20,000, then 10% is $200. To be perfectly honest, it's really hard to make substantial money on the day if you're only working with $200 per day. Don't get me wrong—you CAN make money with $200 per day, you just won't be making BIG money each day playing with that size.

I've talked about how I'm happy if I make over 10% on my trades each day. 10% of $200 is $20. Obviously, $20 per day is not going to make you rich. But *over time,* if you keep on trading smart and winning... before you know it, that $20 per day will add up to $400 in a month. And now you've got a trading account worth $2,400. Now you can spend $240 per day while still following the 10% rule. You can see where I'm going with this.

Over time, if you keep on trading the same way, using the same size on each trade- you will make money and your account size will snowball, slowly but surely. Of course you'll lose on some trades, but with my strategy you'll be winning approximately 70-80% of the time, whether you risk $200 or $2,000 each day.

So now, if you're a reader with a smaller sized trading account *(under 5K)*, you're forced to ask yourself a question: Do you want to play it safe and take LONGER to build up your account, or trade more aggressively by risking a larger portion of your total account in the hopes of making a larger return each day?

You might remember back in chapter 6 when we talked about the motivations of FEAR and DESIRE. This comes into play right now. Are you willing to accept more risk because of your desire to make larger profits quicker, or do you want to play it safe because you don't want to risk your capital?

That's a question only you can answer. I would encourage you to take the safer route... but we're all adults here, and it's your money—so just take this information and do with it what you will.

THE MANY FACES OF RISK

Remember, risk doesn't only factor into your trading when you're deciding how much size to play with, or where you decide to stop out if the trade goes against you. Risk is actually a continuous element that is active throughout the entirety of your trade, from open to close.

People think about certain *actions* of trading in relation to certain *phases* of trading. So a person might think, *"Managing risk happens when I figure out what size to play with before I enter a position, and then when to get out if the trade goes against me."* But in reality, how you manage the trade *from open to close* has an effect on how much risk you assume over the life of that trade.

What do I mean by this? Let's say for example you're in a short position with 10 contracts, and price is steadily falling, so you're winning. As the price drops you need to decide when to exit, and how quickly to exit. Will you sell all 10 contracts at the first sign of profit? Will you hold onto all 10 contracts until it looks like the trend is all but exhausted? Or will you gradually sell your contracts 1 or 2 at a time and try to 'ride the wave' of price action as it falls?

How you play this has a direct impact on your P&L for the day. Sometimes it would have been best to sell all at once. Sometimes it would have been better to hold on for longer. But you'll only know what would have been THE BEST option after the session is over and you review how the action turned out on the day. As they say, hindsight is 20/20, and this is definitely true in trading.

Each day we can look at the way the charts turned out and say, *"I should have done that..."* It's extremely rare to have what you would consider to be the 'perfect' trade. You'll always look back at your trades in hindsight and realize that you could have made more had you done this, or you would have lost less had you done that... and this is why it's so important to NOT get hung up on trading perfectly. Trading itself is an imperfect art. Get used to it and accept it.

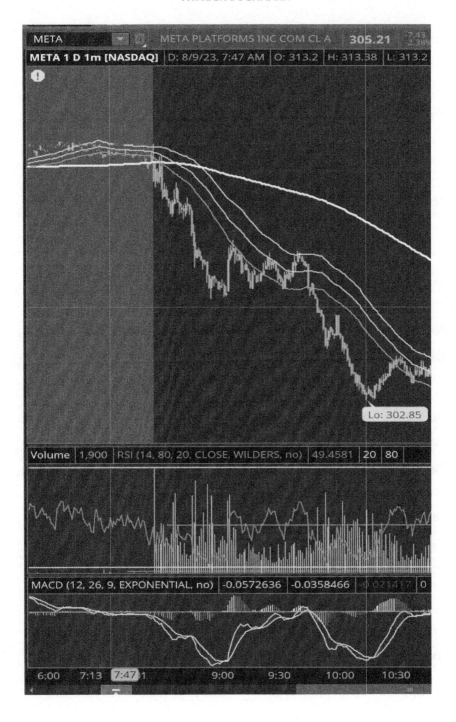

Today, as I write this, META opened at about 313, and by 10 minutes into the session price was at about 310. So in just 10 minutes, you would have made around 3 points on the trade. This 3 point move could have netted you hundreds of dollars with just a few contracts.

For the next 10 minutes after that *(20 minutes into the session)* price consolidated and looked like it could even reverse and break higher. There were no solid signals to confirm this, but the strength of the downward *trend* had shifted from strong to weak. At this point, if your main objective is to mitigate risk, it's a good idea to get out and lock in your profits. You don't know what the price will do in the future, but you DO know that right NOW, you're holding a 3 point gain.

If your main objective is not to mitigate risk but rather to be aggressive and really squeeze maximum profits out of the trade, you'd want to keep it open and ride it out. By keeping the trade open, you are assuming the risk that a reversal could happen soon. As it happened today, price continued to fall and reached it's daily low around 2 hours into the trading session.

6 points in 30 minutes on any trade is great. And if you had actually stuck in the trade for the first 2 hours of the day, you would have made nearly 10 points, which is MASSIVE. This one trade alone would have made you thousands of dollars, even with relatively small size.

In this particular case, in hindsight we see that it would have been much better to keep the trade open, wait an extra 10 minutes and make 6 points instead of 3, *or* stick with it for 2 hours and make a whopping 10 points on the trade. Are you willing to sit in front of your screen for 2 hours to make 10 points? I sure as hell am.

And it's actually easier than you might think. But of course, it always comes back to *your* individual tolerance for risk. Only you can decide how much size to go in with at the beginning, and only you can decide how aggressive you want to be when managing your trade.

As I just said, it's EXTREMELY rare to have what I consider the 'perfect' trade. At this point, about 80% of my trades are winners. And even now when I look back on those winning trades, I'll always see something I could have done better. To think that you'll get in on the perfect minute candle and then exit at the perfect minute candle is unrealistic. But that doesn't mean you won't make tons of money even with imperfect trades.

In nearly every one of my winning trades, I *could have* squeezed out an even larger profit, had I exited a few minutes sooner or later, but you know what? I don't care. A WINNING TRADE IS A WINNING TRADE. That doesn't mean I'm saying, *"Don't study the trade"* I always want you to study your trade, win or lose. What I'm saying is: if you're winning, first be happy that you won and *then* analyze everything to see what you could have done even better.

To wrap up my thoughts on risk, just remember this:

- **More aggressive trade management equals more risk, and more risk equals LARGER gains *and* losses.**

- **A profit or loss is *always* theoretical until you close the position. Once you close the position, the outcome is final and your gains *or* losses are real.**

- **You will very rarely have 'the perfect trade', and that's OK. A winning trade is a winning trade.**

CHAPTER 14

Dealing With Losing

"The greatest glory in living lies not in never falling, but in rising every time we fall." —Nelson Mandela

Losses are a GOOD THING. Now before you close this book and throw it across the room, hear me out. I have learned MORE from every red trade I've made than from any green trade. I've learned more from losing trades than from anything I've read, from any videos I've watched, or from anyone I've personally talked to. Studying losses that happen directly TO YOU is absolutely the best way to become a better trader.

You may remember being a little kid and asking your parents to explain what death means. If they actually attempted to answer the question rather than just brushing you off, they probably tried to describe the sadness and loneliness of it. I'll bet you nodded your head and acted like you understood what they were talking about. But of course, you didn't truly understand until you *personally* felt the reality of experiencing death for the first time—usually with your first pet or a grandparent.

Only after that first experience did you *really* know what death was. The same thing goes with love. You can ask anyone to explain what it's like to fall in love, and they'll give you their own unique take on it... which is absolutely meaningless compared to when you actually feel it yourself.

The only time losses aren't a good thing is when you don't learn anything from them. Every loss is an opportunity to learn. Every loss tests your resilience, your willpower, your ability to focus and your ability to handle stress.

Nobody likes losing. It's a serious blow to the ego, especially when your technical analysis tells you that the stock *should have* done this one thing you thought it would do. Stocks will always do whatever they want, no matter how bulletproof your technical analysis is. Obviously I win more often than I lose *(or else I wouldn't have this career & wouldn't be writing this book)*, and I have the ultimate confidence in my abilities and my process—but I know that **winning is never a *guaranteed* outcome.** There's always a chance you'll lose on the trade.

I know I've put a good amount of effort in this book trying to build up your confidence. I've been saying, *"You can do it"* with each chapter, and that's not a lie. I DO believe you can do it. I've done it, and so can you. But you also need to face some hard facts: you WILL take losses in your career. Think about it: the *best to ever do it* have experienced losses.

Although they had the winningest season in NBA history, the Golden State Warriors still lost 9 games in the 2015-16 season *(including the finals!)* Losses happen to the best of us. They are a part of life and a part of trading. DO NOT beat yourself up if you accumulate some losses, even after consecutive daily losses. When you lose, don't take an *emotional* approach in your attempt to fix things, take an *analytical* approach. We're not trying to make the market fall in love with us. We're trying to solve a problem. And when you're trying to solve problems, do you think emotionally, or analytically?

Remember—the losses you take could be substantial. I know this, I've lost thousands on a single trade. There's no shame in losing, as long as you DON'T repeat the same mistakes over and over. I think about the quote by Winston Churchill, *"All men make mistakes, but only wise men learn from their mistakes."* Be wise. Learn from your mistakes. You will get there... maybe not quickly, but eventually. And getting there *eventually* is much better than never beginning the journey.

'Learning your lesson' in trading is bit like the old analogy of having you mother say, *"Don't touch the hot stove!"*... and then of course you touch the hot stove anyway. Your mom's warning wasn't enough to keep you from touching the stove, but the burn you got on your hand after you touched the stove *was* enough to keep you from doing it again.

When you do experience losses, your success or failure moving forward depends 100% on your mindset and your response to those losses.

There are certain negative things you'll just need to experience for yourself. No matter what I, or anyone else tells you, some things need to be experienced firsthand in order to be fully comprehended. I can tell you how much it sucks losing $1,000 on a single trade, and I'm sure you'll believe me, and I'm sure that the thought of it terrifies you… but it's nothing compared to the feeling you'd have if *you* actually lost that $1,000 *yourself.*

Win or learn. That's an old sports reference, and it works perfectly here as well. You won't always win. But you should *always* learn when you don't win.

Remember—you are not a loser if you lose sometimes. You're only a loser if you decide to quit. There have been many times early on in my trading career when I was close to blowing up my account. I never *actually* blew it up, but I whittled it away to just a few hundred dollars a few times. I'd get it back by going on a huge winning streak, and think to myself, *"I've got it,"* only to blow huge amounts once again on more stupid, ill-advised trades because I thought I was invincible.

You don't have to do this. Learn from my mistakes before you make them yourself. Trade smart, trade strategic, trade cold-and-calculating, not emotional.

CHAPTER 15

Dealing With Winning

"Success is not the key to happiness. Happiness is the key to success. If you love what you are doing, you will be successful."—Albert Schweitzer

This chapter will be shorter than the previous one and much more fun to read, because this is what we want: to *win*, day after day. If you're good at this, you'll find yourself racking up a nice, long streak of winning days before you see a losing one. My record streak of winning days is currently at 53. That's right—53 green days before having a red one.

If you find yourself winning day after day *(which you should if you're understanding this book correctly)*, here's the best thing I can tell you—**if it ain't broke, don't fix it.** That's something my dad used to say frequently, and in this case it's very practical advice. If what you're doing is working, resist the temptation to 'change things up' just for the hell of it. Don't think, *"What happens if I add the (insert random indicator here) into the mix?"* The strategy doesn't need you to add your own special sauce in order to work better. Just be happy that you're WINNING, and keep doing what you're doing. You don't get bonus points for innovation here.

The ONE thing you'll eventually need to consider is if and when to scale, but we'll get into how to do that in the next chapter. For now, I want to focus on the psychology of winning. The first thing you MUST do after every win, which is the same thing you do with every loss, is ask yourself, *"WHY did that trade work?"* The WHY of it all. That's the most important thing to keep in mind when reviewing your trades, win *or* lose.

If you make a $1,000 profit on the day don't just think, *"Sweet! I just made a grand today"* And then walk away from the computer. Study the trade. Remember what you saw pre-market. Remember *why* you traded the way you did. You obviously thought you saw something setting up based on your technical analysis and the chart patterns. Is what you *thought* you saw *actually* what happened? Did you get lucky? Was it all due to your own skill? Perhaps a combination of both?

- There are 2 ways to win: luck or skill.

- There are 2 ways to lose: luck or lack of skill.

Sometimes, *both* of these things happen at once. I've had winning trades that I know were due to good luck *(back before I really knew what I was doing)*, and I've had losing trades that I know were due to BAD luck, because when I went back to review the trade, and double checked my analysis and reviewed the chart... my trade *should have* worked, but it didn't. That's the old 'market will do whatever it wants' effect coming into play. Sometimes this just happens. As I've said numerous times already in this book, even the best traders in the world have losing trades.

Just remember this: even though there are always *more* lessons to be learned from losing trades, there's still plenty to learn from winning ones. And just like I'm telling you to avoid thinking, *"I'm a loser"* if you have multiple losing days, don't start thinking you're bulletproof simply because you've racked up an impressive streak of winning days.

Everything can change in a heartbeat, so don't get cocky. Don't start thinking you can slack on your premarket analysis or your technical analysis. Don't let your ego get the best of you. Humility is an endearing trait, and it's one that will help keep you on the right track. Learn to win with grace, just as you would want to lose with grace.

CHAPTER 16

Going Big: How and When to Scale

"The only way to deal with an unfree world is to become so absolutely free that your very existence is an act of rebellion."

— Albert Camus

At this point you should have already experienced 'all the feels' of trading. You've experienced the thrill of winning and the agony of defeat. By now you're well aware of the risks, and the precautions you can take to mitigate risk. You've gotten comfortable with your own emotions, and hopefully you've learned more about yourself in respect to how you deal with stress.

Let's say you were a completely novice trader when you picked up this book, and in a few months from now you'll be making $100 per day. You'll probably feel pretty amazing pulling money out of thin air with a few clicks of a mouse. But there will come a time when $100 per day isn't as exciting to you, and you'll want to make MORE money each day. That's totally understandable. I felt the same thing. But if you want to actually make more money each day, you'll need to scale up, meaning—you'll need to play with more size each day.

I have good news and bad news regarding this process. The GOOD news is: you don't need to do anything different regarding your strategy. You keep on studying the chart patterns in the same way, plotting your support & resistance lines, etc. None of the technical aspects of trading change, whether you're trading 1 contract or 100.

The BAD news is- if you want to shoot for bigger rewards, you'll need to accept more risk. Here's a theoretical example *(in reality you'll rarely find a contract priced EXACTLY at $100):* if you buy one $100 contract and say, *"I'm going to stop out if I lose 10% on the trade"* and the trade goes against you so you stop out for a 10% loss—you will have lost $10 in total. No big deal.

But if you had scaled up and bought 10 contracts at $100 a piece, and you lose on that trade, now when you stop out you've lost $100. A much more substantial amount of money. One thing you can do in order to mitigate huge losses is to adjust your acceptable risk levels based on how much size you're playing with.

If you take that same 10 contract *($1,000 total)* trade, but tighten up your risk tolerance from 10% down to 3%, now if the trade goes against you, you lose $30 and not $100. Much better.

I've been talking about percentages as examples of risk tolerances, but there are many different ways to perceive the amount. You could use a straight-up dollar amount: *"I won't lose more than $10 per trade" (or $20, $40, $100... whatever number you're comfortable with)...* or you could do it visually, which is something I do often.

Rather than simply use dollar amounts or percentages, I like to use support and resistance levels on my charts to know where to get out or where to take profits. And the larger the size I'm playing with, the 'tighter' I'll set my stop loss and profit targets.

Scaling up is not something to be taken lightly. In the beginning of my trading journey, there were multiple times I *thought* I was ready to scale up. I'd be making a few hundred dollars per day, and then when I tried for $500+ dollars per day, I'd get shot down. I had no problem making $100-200 per day, but once I tried to scale, I always experienced losses. And I realized that even though the analysis and the understanding of the charts was the same in both cases *(as far as identifying levels & proper entries)* the management of the trade and the exits needs to change when you're playing with larger size.

Because if you have just 1-3 contracts, a larger move isn't going to affect you as much. For example, if you hold 1 call options contract, you'll make less money on a big push up, but you'll also lose less money on a big wash *(the most you could lose is the price of the 1 contract)* whereas a smaller move will affect you more when you're playing with a larger amount of contracts, since you're leveraged with so many more of the underlying shares due to holding more contracts.

So this means that visually, when I'm looking at a chart I give myself LESS screen real estate as the amount of my contracts increases. I'll give myself a metaphorical 'shorter leash' to work with before I'm out of the position, in order to minimize risk. If I have one call contract that I bought for $100 and the price suddenly falls to $90, I've lost $10. No big deal. I can handle that, and I won't think twice about keeping the position open longer if the charts tell me there's a good chance price will come back in my favor. But now, if I'm holding 20 contracts and the price falls from $100 to $90, I've suddenly lost $200. Still not the end of the world, but I'm definitely going to keep a close eye on it. If the price continues to fall, then before I know it that $200 loss could be a $500 or even $1,000 loss, and then it's serious.

Here are a few more things to consider before you decide to scale up with your size:

- Consistent Profits: Before scaling up, ensure that you have a consistent track record of profitable trades over a reasonable period. Knowing that you're *already* able to consistently generate positive returns is an important prerequisite for scaling up. Don't go big before you're ready.

- Risk Management: Always prioritize risk management. As you scale up, tighten up the risk management levels you followed when trading smaller positions. Set stop-loss orders, define your risk per trade as a percentage or dollar amount of your trading capital, and stick to those limits.

- Gradual Increases: Increase your position size gradually. Avoid sudden jumps in position size, as this can lead to increased emotional stress and potential mistakes. Don't jump from 3 contracts to 30. Go from 3 per day to 5 per day, then 10 per day, then 15, and so on. Make sure you can handle each step of increased size as you progress.

- Market Conditions: Consider market conditions when scaling up. If the market is experiencing heightened volatility or uncertainty *(or a Fed announcement that day)* it's smart to wait for more stable conditions before increasing your position sizes. Also—I always trade smaller size on Fridays because it's weekly expiry day, and each passing minute affects Theta decay more as you run out of time before expiration.

- Stress Testing: Before significantly increasing your position size, consider paper trading with your desired larger size for a week or two and see how that works. This can help you realize if you're ready to scale up with real money.

- Monitor and Adapt: As you scale up, monitor your trading performance closely. If you notice any negative patterns or losses starting to accumulate, either go back to the smaller size you were trading previously, or stick to paper trading the larger size until you're successful.

- Stay Disciplined: Scaling up should not lead to reckless trading. Stick to your trading plan, maintain discipline, and avoid chasing after unrealistic gains. It can be intoxicating thinking about how much more money you could make each day with larger size, but remember—this is a marathon, not a sprint. Success requires developing a process then sticking to that process.

This chapter has been fairly short on purpose: because scaling up is *not* something you should be doing for a while. But eventually you'll get there. And by the time you DO get there, hopefully you won't even need a book to tell you the best way to do it… by that time you'll be a skilled trader in your own right. Just remember: **LARGER SIZE = MORE RISK *AND* MORE REWARD. If you're going to scale, make sure you're ready to scale.** That's the biggest takeaway here.

CHAPTER 17

From Open to Close

"None of you seem to understand. I'm not locked in here with you. You're locked in here with me." — Rorschach

Here we are, nearing the home stretch. We've already covered everything from your entry, to managing the trade, to closing your position—so by now you should understand all phases of the trade and feel comfortable from opening to closing. Now I want to take you through a trade step-by-step and show you how to spot trends, interpret candlestick patterns and deal with the price action as it develops.

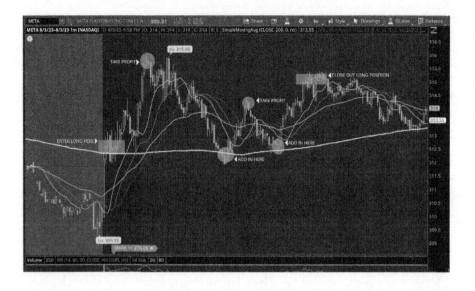

This particular trade is on META. First, focus on the premarket area of the image *(the light grey shaded box on the left)*. We can see it under the 200 EMA just before the market opens. I'm not planning to get involved right at the open, because there hasn't been enough substantial directional movement to make me lean in either direction *(long or short)*... it was moving slightly downward in premarket, but premarket volume is a fraction of what normal daily volume is, so any premarket directional trends aren't nearly as significant as market hours trends are. Based on what you see premarket, you may be tempted to go short right at the open, but this would be a mistake, and you'll quickly see why. I'll need to see it break hard in either direction *after* the market opens before I'll have any confidence in where the price is heading. Remember, my strategy is based on identifying *trends,* so **no trend, no trade.**

You can see there's a GIANT green candle in the very first minute of the open, but I'm waiting because price hasn't broken above the 200 EMA yet. It's too easy to get 'faked out' in this situation—you'll think it's about to rip because of the first candle, but then it *could* still fail… so I'm sitting it out until I see legit conformation. In the 4th minute of the day, we see a sizable red candle that pushes price downward. This is the 'make or break' moment for META. If the stock is truly weak, then price will retreat back to at least the pre-market lows, where it was just a few minutes before the open. If I saw that, I'd go short.

But as you can see, the price doesn't retreat, it just rides the 200 EMA for a few minutes and then pushes *above* it… so in the 7th or 8th minute *(where the first oval highlight is)* that's where I'd have confidence that we're heading higher. I'd then cross reference the MACD and the RSI indicators to make sure I don't see any divergent signals which would make me hesitate… and if those 2 indicators confirm the trend then I would buy some call options at the 312.5 strike price *(the closest strike to ATM that's available at that time).*

This moment in the trade is where the 'art' of the strategy comes into play, and this is something that can only be developed with experience. A person with 10 days of trading experience will simply NOT see the candles or chart patterns the same way a person with 10 years trading experience will see them.

And this is why daily repetition is so important. We want to get involved in the trade *as close to the beginning of the trend* as we possibly can—but we also want to make sure it's a real trend and not a fake out. And the only way to really hone that skill is to look at the same charts, day after day. Whether you get involved or not, you should still be viewing the same charts on the same time frames, every day. Remember that Bruce Lee quote I referenced earlier: *"I don't fear the man who's practiced 10,000 kicks once... I fear the man who's practiced 1 kick 10,000 times."* This is our version of practicing the same kick 10,000 times.

OK, back to price action. Let's say I've just bought five call option contracts at a strike price of 312.5 at the 7th minute of the day when I realized price was holding on above the 200 EMA. I will set my stop out level at 311 *(that small plateau of price just a few minutes before the open)*—so if the trade doesn't work and price action goes against me, I would hold on until price fell to the 311 level. If price does what I expect it will do, and continues to rise, I'll plan on selling 1 or 2 of my contracts on each big push upwards.

Take a look at the two BIG green candles around minutes 18-20. This is the first area where I'd start peeling off my contracts—If I opened the position with 5 contracts I would sell one at each large green candle. If I started with 10 contracts I would sell 2 or 3 at each push.

I'm closing about 40% of my total size here because I don't want to get completely flat yet *('flat' meaning no more open contracts)* but I *do* want to lock in a bit of profit, as insurance. Remember, **the gain or loss is only 'realized' once you close the trade.** From the moment you open your position, all of your P&L is theoretical until you close that position. That's why having a perfectly timed exit is so important. The passage of just a few seconds can be the difference between making 12% or 15% on a trade.

Notice the big red engulfing candle right next to the green candle that says 'HI: 315.95'. This is a spot where many novice traders would get freaked out and sell their remaining contracts, thinking a wash out is about to happen. In hindsight, if you *did* simply close the rest out here you would have still made money on the trade, so that's fine.

But I don't want to close out the rest here, for a few reasons. First, we can see at that moment that our indicators are fully bullish in the way they're 'stacked'... you can see price sitting above the Alligator's lips, which is above the 50 EMA, which is above the 200 EMA. These pieces of visual information make be think the trend still has plenty of room to work.

The next 30 minutes or so are scary. You WILL have moments like this every day, when you feel like you're just hanging on for dear life in the trade as you watch your P&L evaporating minute-by-minute.

You can see about 20 minutes after the HI: 315.95 mark, it looks like we could have a small double bottom setting up... but the part that *should have* bounced off the 50 EMA to create the bottom right point of the 'W' washes out instead. It would be understandable if you closed out some of your position here, because that's *not* a good sign.

But we do have an ace in the hole, and this is why I would still be holding here... the 200 EMA. Based on what I've seen so far up until that moment, I believe price will bounce off the 200 EMA if it gets that low. Why? Because of the way price just *ripped* through the 200 as soon as the market opened. It's not like it was just riding the 200 for a while—it sliced through the level like a hot knife through butter. This makes me believe that the 200 EMA will be a strong support level at this moment.

And as you can see, it DOES act as a strong support level. Right at the large green candle to the left of 'add in here', this is indeed where you should add in if you have conviction that your original idea was correct. I DO believe my original idea was correct so I would add here. I've already locked in profits from about 40% of my original size, and so by adding more contracts here I'm just maximizing gains by having more contracts to close after price continues to move in my favor.

About 10 minutes after we've added in to our position, we can see the red engulfing candle that sits just to the right of the green candle where it says 'take profit'. YES, you should take profits here. Price has just climbed steadily for the last 10 minutes, but now I can spot a potentially worrying sign on the chart that's just developed. Do you see it?

Trend formation. We've been making lower highs *(a bearish sign)*, and this latest lower high represents the second lower high we see after the 315.95 mark *(the first one coming about 13 minutes after the high mark)*. This makes me believe price will fall again, at least until we get back to the 200 EMA, which I *still* believe to be a strong support level.

Fast forward about 15 minutes, and we're back down at the 200 again… and like I suspected, the support is STRONG. On that huge green candle just left of 'add in here'… you guessed it! We will again ADD to the position, because it's obvious the 200 will once again hold, and we've established a healthy double bottom *(if you can't see the giant 'W' staring at you, perhaps visit your optometrist)*. I will add here for the last time of the day, and hope to ride this back up above the level where the 'take profit' candles are.

Fast forward another 15 minutes. At this point, we can see that price action looks like it's consolidating. It's no longer trending up or down, it's basically moving sideways. I would definitely close out my remaining positions here for a profit.

Why here? Three reasons. First, the obvious sideways movement of price action is what I don't want to see. As I've stated before, sideways action is the kiss of death for the way I trade. I want price moving UP or DOWN, never sideways. Secondly, the level where we're consolidating is *below* the highs of the day, which leads me to believe we may not have the juice to push higher.

If price had pushed *above* the previous highs and then consolidated, I might feel like it's just 'taking a breath' before continuing it's upward climb, but to settle below the day's previous high has me less confident. Last but not least, at this point we would have been in the trade for over an hour, and usually I like to round-trip a trade in less than an hour.

The beauty of trading the way I do is that you can make money NO MATTER WHAT happens in the market that day, as long as you can spot the trends and identify chart patterns correctly. When other investors are freaking out because of a huge red day, you've just made thousands of dollars because you saw the signs and bought put options. Your success doesn't rely on the market doing any *one* specific thing. The market can do whatever it wants to every day, and as long as you see things correctly, you can profit from it.

Hopefully by this time you understand and believe in my strategy, and you're getting a good grasp of how all of the pieces fit together. But just in case you still have doubts about the real world application of it, below I've included my P&L and the 1-minute charts from an actual day of trading I had recently, in which I made $1,000 (24% *gains*) in 30 minutes. I traded 18 contracts—which is not exactly 'small' size, but it's not *huge* either. If you have at least $3,000 in your account you could trade like this.

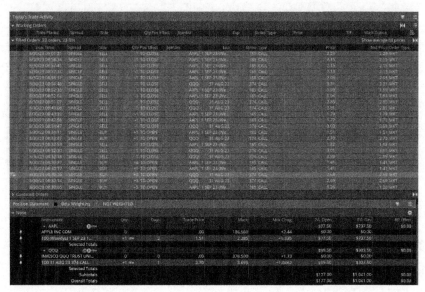

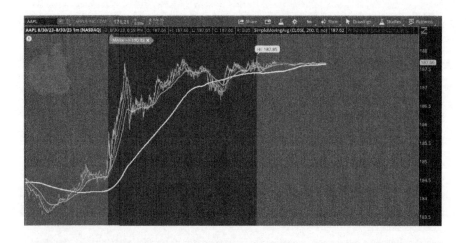

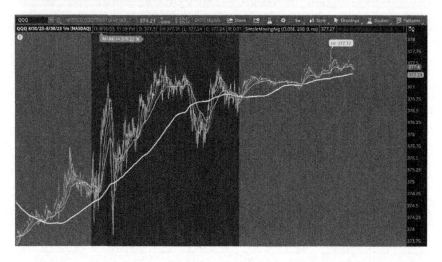

You can see that this happened on August 30, 2023. That date is clearly visible on the order entries and also on the charts of AAPL and QQQ, and you can look for yourself online at any chart for 08/30/23 and you'll see the same thing. On this particular day I got in with size right at the first minute of the day, which is something I don't usually do—but you can see how price for both AAPL and QQQ was steadily trending up during premarket, and then had a little flag right before the open, but the indicators were still stacked bullish.

This made me think price would rip to the upside right at the open, which is exactly what happened. I got in *quickly* and captured almost the entire move until the peak reversal right around 9AM CST. Notice how I scaled in and out of these trades. A majority of my buys were at the very first minute of the open, but then I added in 5 minutes later when I saw that my initial idea was correct. I closed a couple of contracts 2 minutes after the open just for some insurance *(locking in the profits)*, and then from 8:34 to 9:00 AM I slowly and steadily scaled out of my position, one contract at a time, until I was out completely at 9:01 AM.

Not all days develop this cleanly, and of course I've had losing days. Anyone who tells you they never lose is straight-up lying to you. The point is, it *can* be this easy... and although it's rarely as cut-and-dried perfect as the example above, trust me—it works at least 70% of the time. A 70% success rate is a number I can live with.

CHAPTER 18

Putting it All Together

"One must still have chaos in oneself to be able to give birth to a dancing star."—Friedrich Nietzsche

Congratulations! You're now well on your way to becoming a successful trader. You are no longer a cog in someone else's machine, but the pilot of your *own* machine—the one that you built with nothing more than the power of your own mind.

Once you experience the absolute joy of making money on your own terms, you'll wonder how you were ever able to work as an employee for so many years. In this chapter I want to re-iterate a few super important aspects of trading by giving you some 'golden rules' to remember, and summarize the previous chapters of this book. So even though you *should have* read every page until now, you can just use this chapter as a quick reference.

NOW THAT YOU KNOW WHAT YOU'RE DOING, LET'S SUMMARIZE YOUR DAY-TO-DAY ACTIVITIES, IN CHRONOLOGICAL ORDER.

- PRE MARKET: Do technical research every morning and look for valid levels based on where the stock price has been <u>recently</u>, on both the daily chart and the 1-minute chart *(including pre-market action)*. Create alerts at those valid levels. This is where you'll look to enter—either long or short. Establish the strike prices that you'll buy if the stock triggers your alerts and establishes a mature trend in either direction. Add your strike prices to your watchlist, which is linked to your BUY MKT and SELL MKT buttons in your top right window. Make sure 'auto send' is checked so there will be NO delay in your order when you place it.

- MARKET OPENS: Stay hyper focused on each individual 1-minute candle of your chart(s). Do not try to pay attention to more than 2 or 3 different stocks at any one time. The more focused your attention is, the more 'locked in' you'll be as you examine that stock's price action. I usually choose 1 or 2 that I'll be looking at pre-market, and only shift my focus to others if an alert triggers. When you see an alert trigger, that's the time to *really* focus in on that stock, to make sure it's actually the right time to enter.

- ENTER THE TRADE: When you have valid confirmation from multiple sources that a trend has established itself *(long or short)* look for a slight pullback to enter. For example: if you're going long, look for the first red candle or the bottom wick on a green candle to enter. Even if you only gain a few cents per contract with an excellent entry, this can definitely add up if you're using size. Every dollar counts, so watch the 1 minute chart for the 'perfect' time to enter.

- MANAGE THE TRADE: Have profit targets and stop loss levels set, and pay attention to them. Stay in as long as you can while you're still gaining profits. If the trend is working in your favor, ride it until the strength of the trend starts to wane. Don't trade with fear or greed. Remember your ability to 'add in' to the trade whether you're winning or losing. If you're winning, adding-in can get you even bigger profits. If you're losing and you have confidence that your original idea was correct, adding in can 'fix' your average price by lowering the price of each contract. Don't add-in unless you have strong confidence in the validity of the trade. Use your indicators and identify chart patterns to help determine the strength or weakness of the trend.

- EXIT THE TRADE: Once you're in a trade, use your profit or stop loss targets to determine the timing of your exits. If you're winning, close individual contracts one-by-one as big pushes happen. If you're losing, wait until you *actually reach* your stop loss level before you finally get out. Don't get freaked out and close too early if you're losing, and don't get greedy and hold on too long if you're winning. Just like how you look for the 'perfect' entry point based on the 1 minute chart, you also look for the 'perfect' exit based on the 1-minute chart. If you're in long, wait for the top tick of green candle wicks to sell. If you're in short, look for the bottom wicks of red candles to sell.

- STUDY THE TRADE: When you're finished trading for the day, look at the charts and compare them to your entries and exits. Take this moment to go back and study everything you did. Do you still see the same things that you saw on the charts when you were in the trade, or do you see things differently now that your position is closed? Make a list of everything that worked, and everything that didn't work for you, and then make a list of all the things you could have done better that day. Remember—even when you lose on the day, you're only a loser once you decide to quit. If you did lose, try to determine—was the problem mental, or technical? And if you won—did you win because of luck, or your own skill? (*or maybe a bit of both?)* Use all of the insights you gained today to trade even better tomorrow.

A FEW 'GOLDEN RULE' CONCEPTS OF THE LONE WOLF TRADING STRATEGY:

THE MARKET WILL DO WHAT IT WANTS, WHENEVER IT WANTS

This is the most important insight you can take away from this book. It's as true as the laws of time and space. If you're not OK with a certain amount of risk, then day trading is NOT for you. There WILL be times when you LOSE money. Accept that fact, and get comfortable with it. I am living proof *(as are many other full-time, professional traders)* that you CAN make a great living doing this as a full time career, but don't ever think you'll avoid losses. The greatest technical analysis on the planet won't be correct 100% of the time.

THE TREND IS YOUR FRIEND

This concept is the 'heart and soul' of my trading style. **Identify a valid trend, jump in, ride that trend until it weakens, then close the position for a profit.** It's as simple as that. Sure, you *could* make money being a contrarian trader *(just like you could make money with any style of trading)*, but I've found the safest & most predictable method of trading is going with the trend. Predictability is bad for novels and TV shows... but GREAT for trading. Bruce Lee famously said, *"Be like water."* Listen to Bruce and let your trading flow along in the same direction as the chart is moving. Don't wait too long to get in, or else you'll miss the biggest part of the move. But ALSO, don't be afraid to take the trade just because you didn't get in at the exact beginning of the move.

ALWAYS TRADE THE CHART, NOT YOUR FEELINGS

What this means is—don't trade based on, *"I've got a feeling"*... trade exactly what you see in front of you, right NOW. For example: When price is above the Alligator indicator, which is above the 50 EMA, which is above the 200 EMA, you ONLY go long. And if you see the same thing but reversed, you ONLY go short. And remember that the steeper the grade of the EMA lines is, the stronger the trend is. Last but not least, the more open the 'mouth' of the Alligator indicator is *(whether it's trending up or down)* the stronger the trend is.

The ONLY exception to this rule is if the trend has *already* been going strong for a while *(over 20-30 minutes)*. When this is the case, it's better to wait for the current trend to exhaust itself and look for a reversal *(with confirmation)*, and get in *at the beginning* of the NEW trend. If you only remember these few concepts, you'll be successful more often than not.

FOCUS ON THE FIRST 30-60 MINUTES OF THE SESSION

For the way I trade, volatility is my friend. And the MOST volatility of each day occurs during the first hour of the session. Of course there are days when mid-day action gets wild, but as a general rule, the biggest swings in the shortest amount of time happen in the first hour, and that's why I always concentrate on trading the first 60 minutes of the day. If you simply can't trade the first hour of the session because of work, family or other conflicts, don't worry—you can make money ANY time of the day.

The level of volatility usually won't be as high after the first 60 minutes, but as long as you're identifying the trend and using my strategy, you'll have a same chances of success at 2PM as you would at 10AM. One important caveat regarding early entries: In the first 5-10 minutes of the day, a lot of automatic buy or sell orders will be triggered based on morning gaps, so keep your size down until you're really sure that the action is due to active trading for *that* day, not just automatic orders triggering due to gaps first thing in the morning.

CONFIRMATION=CONFIDENCE

Remember that candlestick patterns don't exist in a vacuum. Identify the 'bigger picture' by confirming what you you see on the charts with your indicators. The more types of confirmation you find to back up your trade idea, the more confidence you can have in making the trade. I never make a move if I only have one source of information. I like to confirm with at least 3 or 4 different sources before I enter or exit any position.

THE POWER OF NOW

The closer we are to the time frame of 'now' when we trade, the more predictability we have in the price action. This is why ideally I like to have all of my trades round-tripped within an hour. It's a balancing act between trying to squeeze the MAXIMUM move out of a trend, while also getting out completely before that trend exhausts itself and reverses. It's easy in hindsight to see when you should have stayed in longer, or exited sooner. You won't always nail it perfectly... but remember, you don't have to be perfect—as long as you're *close* with both your entry and exit, you'll still make money.

SEE THE CHARTS AS ART

Do not focus on numbers, statistics, graphs, etc. See the charts as *art*. Notice the patterns on the screen. The better you can visually identify multiple patterns on different time frames and then analyze their unique relationships to each other, the more valid information you'll have in your mind as you predict the next move. Trading is chess, not checkers.

COMPARE MULTIPLE TIME FRAMES

You always have to think multiple moves ahead, and the best way to do that is to see as much as possible on the screen. And when I say 'see as much as possible' I'm not talking about simply adding more indicators, I'm talking about viewing price action over different time frames. You might see a certain pattern developing on the 1 hour chart, but something completely different developing on the 15 minute chart. Don't simply look at the charts and think, *"Here's what it is."* Look at the charts and ask yourself, *"What does it mean?"* View one ticker on multiple time frames, and try to decipher the meaning to the different patterns that emerge on each time frame.

DO NOT TRADE BASED ON THE NEWS

99% of the information you should be paying attention to is right there in front of you on the chart. I know it's tempting to watch CNBC and say to yourself, *"Kramer says that (insert ticker here) is going to the moon!"* Most financial news is effectively background noise in respect to the way I trade. Sure, it has significance to somebody somewhere, but not me. Don't pay too much attention to the news. When there's a

Fed meeting, or earnings, then SIZE DOWN in your trades, since Fed announcements introduce uncertainty into the trading day. News announcements might affect the size I'll use—but never *the way* I trade.

ONE AND DONE

One of the worst habits to develop is over-trading. If you're trading 5 different tickers every day, that's TOO MUCH trading. If you set a very narrow stop and then flip from long to short, and then back again in the course of one day, that's TOO MUCH TRADING. I like to wait until I see a mature trend develop, and then take the ride, whichever way it's going *(long or short)*. Most days I'll just take that one trade, ride it until it loses steam, cash out and I'm done for the day. Occasionally, if it looks like there's a very defined reversal that happens, I'll cash out of my first position and then flip the other way to open a new position, which could take me into the afternoon or even the end of the day before I close it—but that's rare. The most volatile action of the day usually happens in the first hour, so that's when I like to do most of my trading.

TRADE FOR PERFECTION, AND THE MONEY WILL FOLLOW

Don't trade to make money, trade to trade perfectly. Of course, there's no such thing as 'the perfect trade', but that's not the point. When I trade, I'm attempting to trade perfectly. You might be 100% focused on WINNING, and that's OK too. But for me personally, if I focus on *winning* then I'm always thinking about the extra money I could have made had I done this or that differently... but when I focus on 'trading perfection' then it's more about the daily journey itself than the P&L, and taking a journey is a more beautiful thing than simply making money.

LOOK FOR MATURITY

Don't jump the gun when you're looking for entries. Make sure the trend you've identified is actually mature to avoid being 'faked out' by false breakouts or reversals. Obviously we want to be in as early as possible when trends develop, but make sure you don't get in before there really *is* a mature trend. This is all about having the correct timing. Just like it's important to not get scared and wait too long to enter, it's also important to wait until the trend is *real* before you jump in. By now, you should know the signs to look for to determine whether a trend is valid, so make sure you actually *do that* rather than just jumping into a position because you got too excited by one candle.

CONTROL YOUR EMOTIONS

Don't trade based on feelings. DO NOT succumb to either greed or fear. Trade based on the charts. All the information you need is right in front of you. If you find yourself saying, *"I've got a feeling that…"* STOP. Do not trade feelings. Trade data. All the data you need is right in front of your eyes. If you wake up in the morning and say to yourself, *"I feel like it's going to be a bullish day today"* but then when you check the charts all you see is bearish trending, *obviously* you would want to go short and be on the right side of the trend. Don't try to outsmart the market. Simply observe where the market is going and stay on the right side of the move.

MIND THE FED, EARNINGS AND FRIDAYS

Always size down whenever there's a Fed announcement, or when there are earnings coming up within the next week on a particular ticker. I like to go about 1/4 size for either of these occasions, so for example: if your 'normal' trading size is 20 contracts per day, on Fed announcement days or the week of earnings you'd trade 5 contracts per day. Also, always scale down on Fridays because that's expiry day, and with no time left on your contract, Theta decay is more prominent. I like to *definitely* be round-tripped within the first hour of the day on Fridays.

So to summarize the previous 16 chapters:

CHAPTER 1: First things first

The MOST IMPORTANT thing you need is a mindset that is confident and full of self-belief. Without confidence, you will not be able to trade well. You need to *believe you can do this* before you actually try to do this.

You don't need to know everything there is to know about the stock market *or* options to make a six-figure per year income working about 5 hours per week day trading stock options. Using my strategy which involves a specific combination of candlestick charts, time frames and indicators to identify trends in the stock market, you CAN be successful. Remember, you only need to get skilled at ONE particular type of trading, and then trade in that one style consistently, day after day.

CHAPTER 2: The Big Picture

No, you DON'T need a wall of monitors in order to trade successfully. You need a computer, ONE monitor, the fastest internet speed you can get, and your trading software. That's it. Having the fastest internet speed is more important than having the latest & greatest computer. I made tons of money using a bare-bones MacBook Air laptop and a $79 Walmart monitor, and so can you. There are many different trading platforms available *(some paid, some free)*, and most of them work well. I'm using Think or Swim from TD Ameritrade, so I recommend that if you want to be able to configure your setup to look *exactly* like mine.

CHAPTER 3: Hardware and Software

I arrange my external monitor to the left of my computer, and I arrange 2 charts of equal size on that external monitor. The far left chart on my monitor is the 1 minute chart, and the one to the right of that is the 15 minute chart on the same ticker *(although sometimes I'll use dual 1-minute charts here, if I'm trading 2 stocks at one time)* I use a second external monitor on the right side, but this monitor is far less important to me than the left one. If you're a new trader the second monitor is unnecessary.

I glance at my right monitor sometimes to get extra confirmation of a trend by putting up additional charts of the ticker I'm trading that day, but with different time frames. If you want to use 2 external monitors you can set the extra monitor to view either the daily charts or the 5 minute Heiken Ashi charts of the same tickers you're watching on your MAIN external monitor. But remember—this is purely optional. You don't *need* 2 external monitors… just one.

CHAPTER 4: The Set-Up

You don't need the latest & greatest computer—just a fast internet connection and one external monitor. I use Think Or Swim by TD Ameritrade as my brokerage, but there are many other decent options available. Do the research and find which one has the features you like best, or just get TOS if you want your screen & charts setup to look exactly like mine. Take the time to get well acquainted with the Japanese candlesticks. Learn their patterns, both individual candlesticks, and patterns of candlesticks together. Add these 6 indicators to your charts:

1. **200 EMA**

2. **Williams Alligator**

3. **50 EMA**

4. **MACD**

5. **RSI**

6. **Daily High/Low**

You can also check the Keltner Channels and Pivot Points for extra confirmation. I don't use either of those indicators as main sources of information, but they can be helpful to double check when you think you're seeing something develop and just want to see where your idea fits in relation to those indicators.

For example: If you think that price has hit a valid support or resistance level based on what the candlesticks and your main indicators are telling you... perhaps throw up the pivot points and see where price sits in relation to it. If price is sitting right there on a pivot point, that can give you even more confidence that what you *think* you're seeing is actually correct. Remember, never trade based on ONE piecc of information—always get multiple sources of information before you make any moves.

CHAPTER 5: My Daily Routine

This is my daily routine, in a nutshell:

1. Wake up at 8AM *(30 minutes before market open in CST)*

2. Make coffee

3. Fire up the trading machine

4. Study all of my potential tickers for the day *(usually SPY, META, AMD, QQQ and AAPL)*. I look at the daily chart first, then pre-market action

5. Interpret the connection between the pre-market action and the daily chart

6. Place alerts at key levels of support & resistance that determine entry and/or exit points on a trade.

7. Ask myself the question, *"How much money will I make today?"*

8. Wait for the opening bell and start trading

A reminder: The time frames I'm using on my charts are: 1 minute Japanese candlesticks on my external monitor, and 15 and 30 minute Heiken Ashi candlesticks on my main laptop *(or desktop)* screen. If I'm using a second monitor I will frequently switch between the 5 minute, 1 hour and daily charts on that one.

CHAPTER 6: The Proper Mindset

Here's the correct arc of your trading journey:

1. DO NOTHING BUT WATCH the charts for weeks or months until you feel like you 'get' what you're looking at.

2. Do some paper trading for a short amount of time — just long enough to get your sense of timing. Figure out where to look on your screens, where and when to click for your entries *(and the same thing for your exits)*. Get comfortable with the physical process of trading.

3. Once you get the hang of things through paper trading, move into real trading sooner rather than later. Spend much less time trading paper than you did when you were simply watching the charts.

Paper trading is a bit like the first time you got behind the wheel when you were learning to drive…you probably drove around an empty parking lot for a while before you took the car out on the street. Paper trading is the metaphorical 'empty parking lot' here. As soon as you're confident, move into the street and join the traffic.

We trade short time frames, because the closer to NOW we exit, the more predictability we have in where the price will be. Trade in the NOW, not in the past or future. The key to success with my style of trading is to join the trends *as they're happening*. Always try to enter as close to *the start* of a trend as possible, and always try to exit as close to *the end* of the trend as possible.

ALWAYS go into a trade with the mindset, *"I'm going to win in this trade."* Remember, **It's OK to lose in a trade. It's never OK to *think* you're about to lose *before* you enter the trade.**

Don't let financial news disproportionately affect the way you trade. It's OK to stay abreast of financial news, but when you're actually trading— trade the chart, not the news.

DESIRE and FEAR: these are the 2 primary emotional motivations for everything. Neither one is inherently positive or negative—they both have their proper place. But always think about which one of them is driving you as you trade. The more you know yourself, the better you'll trade.

CHAPTER 7: What to trade?

My strategy is based on *trend trading,* which in my opinion is the most predictable & stable way to generate consistent profits. There are other strategies that I've cherry-picked certain elements from, but FOLLOWING THE TREND is at the heart of what I do. The success of the strategy relies on being able to read the candlesticks and predict trends by interpreting the data I get from various indicators.

I use a limited array of indicators on my charts, the most important being the 50 and 200 EMA's, the Alligator Indicator, the MACD and the RSI. I also use a daily high/low indicator which gives me a visual reference of how the previous day's price action relates to the current day's price action. Previous day's high or low can act as a support or resistance level. Sometimes I will also cross reference Keltner Channels or Pivot Points to gain further confirmation about certain levels.

Don't get hung up on researching hundreds of different tickers every day. You only need to watch a handful of blue chip stocks, like META, AAPL, AMD, NVDA, INTC, etc. I also like to trade ETF's like SPY or QQQ. You want to trade blue-chip stocks that have a lot of liquidity so you'll never have a problem getting in or out with a market order.

I only trade using market orders. If you trade using limit orders, you might not get your order filled immediately, and when we pull the trigger on an option we want it to get filled ASAP. Even a few seconds delay could make a big difference on your P&L.

CHAPTER 8: The Process

I never buy or sell individual shares of stock. I buy *stock options.* One options contract controls 100 shares of the underlying stock. This allows me to use more leverage in trades to create bigger profits. But remember—it's not a one-way street. With the ability to make bigger profits also comes the possibility of bigger losses, so be sure you're familiar with the entire process of trading before you trade with any size.

This is why simply WATCHING THE CHARTS for a while before you even attempt a trade is super important. What you see on your screen needs to look *extremely familiar* to you before you risk any of your real, hard earned money in a trade. If you find yourself seeing things on your screen that make you think, *"What is that?"* or, *"What does that mean?"* Then you're *not* ready to trade yet. When you're a beginner the charts will look like a foreign language. Make sure the charts look like a language you visually understand before you actually start trading.

And once you DO start to understand what you're seeing on the charts, you can graduate to paper trading. At this point it's not about simply understanding what you see on screen—you need to *react* to what you see and place trades based on what you see. When you're paper trading you aren't using real money—so all profits or losses are theoretical.

Even though you're not trading real money at this point, you should still trade with the same size you will be using when you *do* graduate to using your own money. What's the point of paper trading $100,000 if you'll only have $2,000 to trade with in real life? Everything about trading with those 2 wildly different amounts is incongruous. Keep it realistic.

A few guidelines while trading:

- I ONLY use Market orders, never limit orders. Market orders allow you to open and close your position quicker than any other type of order. And since I only trade large-cap options with LOTS of liquidity, there's never a problem getting in or out of my position with lightning speed. This is obviously what we want, since every second counts while day trading.

- I almost always choose the closest ITM *(in-the-money)* strike price to ATM *(at-the-money)* options that are available at the time. The ATM strike price will be the closest one to the middle of the box here. There are particular times when I would choose a different strike price, but those times rely on particular things happening that I won't get into here. For most situations, simply **choose the closest ITM to the ATM strike price that's available when you enter.**

- ALWAYS close your position *before* expiration. If you fail to do this and your position is profitable upon expiration you might get assigned, which means your broker automatically buys the amount of underlying shares relating to the amount of contracts you held upon expiration. For example: if you are holding 3 open contracts on AAPL upon expiration and you get assigned, that means your broker would purchase 300 shares of AAPL stock with funds from your account, for the price that AAPL was trading at when your option expired. If this happens it's not the end of the world—you can simply wait until the next day and sell those 300 shares to free up your capital again. But obviously this is a hassle, so avoid this happening at all costs.

CHAPTER 9: Entries

This is the step-by-step process I use before I enter into any position each morning:

1. Check the daily chart to identify any significant support/resistance lines, and look for any significant

candlestick patterns that give me a bullish or bearish lean.

2. Observe the 200 and 50 EMA's, and see where price sits in relation to both of them. Is the 50 above or below the 200? Are they trending up or down? If the price, Alligator and both EMA's are all 'stacked' in one direction *(either bullish or bearish)* that's a very strong trending signal.

3. Get confirmation from the volume chart, RSI and MACD that the trend is mature. Once I am satisfied by the level of confirmation I see, I'll look for a slight pullback in price action to get into the trade.

Familiarize yourself with the many different types of patterns that can develop on the 1-minute charts, and look to enter at precise moments on these patterns. For example: entering long at the right lower point of the 'W' when you spot a double bottom pattern, or entering short at the right upper point of the 'M' on a double top.

Remember to use the daily chart to identify valid daily support & resistance levels, but *only* use the 1-minute chart for your actual entries and exits. Also, remember that if you're going long, it's less important if price is above the 50 EMA on the 30 minute or 1 hour chart. It's much more important that the 1-minute chart shows price above the 50

EMA... and the same concept applies if you're going short, but reversed.

CHAPTER 10: Managing the trade

Resist the emotions of fear and greed. Neither of these are good for your trading. If you trade scared then you'll either wait too long before you enter, or you'll close your positions before you give it a chance to work, therefore missing out on profits. If you trade greedy then you'll fail to take profits when you should, and you'll run the risk of blowing your gains simply because you were trying to squeeze a larger move out of the stock than was realistic. Always have valid profit targets and stop loss levels, and stick to them as you trade.

Always consider 'adding in' as you trade, either to generate even bigger profits when the trade is going your way, or to 'fix' your average price if the trade is NOT going your way. You need to have a strong conviction through technical analysis *(never 'a feeling')* that price *will* in fact go in your favor soon. Remember, ONLY ADD IN WHEN YOU HAVE CONFIDENCE. No *(or low)* confidence=no add in.

Avoid distractions at all costs. A distracted trader is a compromised trader. Make sure you're mentally and physically prepared to dedicate 100% of your focus on the trade from open to close. Your trade will only be open from a matter of minutes to a few hours. Avoid multi-tasking or splitting your attention in any way while it's open.

CHAPTER 11: The Art of the Chart

Don't view the charts as data, view them as art. Identify the patterns that develop within the charts, and use those patterns to identify where price action will go next. The market is ALWAYS doing one of three things: rising, falling, or consolidating. When you're able to interpret the charts more like a painting than a spreadsheet, you'll be able to identify which of the three phases the market is operating in.

Remember to always view multiple time frames and put them all together in order to see the bigger picture. Sometimes a market may be rising on one time frame yet falling on another. I've had many days where I've made money going long when it ended up being a red day *(or going short on a green day)* simply because I got in and out before the larger tides shifted. That's another reason to get in and out of trades quickly. You can more easily predict what will happen 15 minutes from now than 5 hours from now.

CHAPTER 12: Exits

Always try to exit as quickly as you can, but AFTER you confidently believe you've captured the majority of the short-term move. You may be thinking, *"He says exit as fast as possible, but he also says wait before you exit. Which one is it?"* It's BOTH. Those two concepts are not mutually exclusive. You DO ideally want to be out as quickly as possible after you enter, but ONLY AFTER you've maximized the move you jumped in on to begin with. You wouldn't have entered if you didn't see a trend developing, so let the trend work as long as it wants to. When you do see the trend weakening *(with confirmation)*, get out ASAP at that moment.

You can either close all of your contracts at once, or close them out slowly. This second option is my preferred way to do it, for 2 reasons. First, as you know—as soon as you close the position, those profits or losses are 'locked in' and and become realized rather than being theoretical *(and therefore in constant flux)* when the position is open. Each time you close a position, you take a bit of risk off the table, which is good. But that also means there's no more room for further gains when the move is going in your favor.

And this brings us to the second point: By slowly peeling off contracts one by one *(or 2x2, 3x3, or whatever, depending on the size you're working with)* then you simultaneously lock in profits slowly, while continuing to gain profits with your contracts that are still open. Of course—the less contracts you have open, the less price fluctuation you'll see with your P&L, so your additional gains will become less dramatic as you scale down your size. This type of exit requires more finesse than simply hitting 'SELL' and unloading all of your contracts—but I believe it's a more effective way of doing it. And just like how you always get confirmation before an entry—you always get confirmation that the trend is over before you exit.

CHAPTER 13: The Game of Risk

Everyone needs to develop their own personal risk tolerance. There's no magic number that works for everyone. There are a variety of methods you can use to set your profit or loss targets, including a dollar amount: *"I'll take profits after I've made $300 today, and I'll stop out if I lose $100."* Or you could use a percentage amount: *"I'll take profits after I've made 10%, or if I lose 3%."* Always make sure you set your stop loss target tighter than your gains target. This way, if you DO lose on the day, you'll lose a lot LESS than you will gain when you're winning. This is the way to set yourself up for consistent success.

Remember that you can set up an automatic stop order or trailing stop order to close your trades in case you aren't able to physically manage the trade from open to close. That way, you can step away from the computer and know that your brokerage will automatically close your positions in case of wild price swings. Obviously this is not suggested—only do this when it's absolutely necessary. The far better option is to be present, in the moment, from the opening to the closing of your trade.

- More aggressive trade management equals MORE RISK, And MORE RISK equals LARGER GAINS OR LOSSES

- A profit or loss is *always* theoretical until you close the position. Once you close the position, the outcome is final and your gains or losses are real

- You will very rarely have 'the perfect trade', and that's OK. A winning trade is a winning trade

CHAPTER 14: Dealing With Losing

This most important thing to take away from this chapter is this one sentence: **The only time losses *aren't* a good thing is when you don't learn anything from them.** Every loss is an opportunity to learn. Every loss tests your resilience, your willpower, your ability to focus and your ability to handle stress. When you DO experience losses (*and you WILL, trust me*), your success or failure from that moment on depends 100% on YOUR mindset and your response to those losses.

Remember—you are not a loser if you lose sometimes. You're only a loser if you decide to quit.

CHAPTER 15: Dealing With Winning

There are 2 ways to win: luck or skill. Obviously, we always want *our* reason for winning to be all skill and no luck, but luck will come into play frequently. And just like you shouldn't think you're a loser if you have multiple losing days, don't start thinking you're a bulletproof genius if you go on a winning streak that lasts days or even weeks. Always stay focused, perceptive and grounded, no matter what your daily outcome is.

CHAPTER 16: Going Big: How and When to Scale

DO NOT scale up until you're ready. I can't stress this enough. Just because you've achieved daily success trading 1-3 contracts per day, the experience of trading 10-20 contracts per day is VERY different, and trading 100 contracts per day is like being in another universe. The price swings become greater and greater as you size up, so you MUST be ready for the psychological reality of seeing a your P&L up $500 one minute and then down $500 just a few minutes later. If you're not ready to experience those massive price fluctuations without a full bottle of Pepto by your side, don't even go there.

I remember when I was nearly passing out if I gained or lost a hundred dollars in a day. Now every gain or loss I see is a lot bigger than that, and it doesn't rattle me at all. Even if I lose hundreds of dollars one day, I know I can make thousands back the next day. This is the mindset you need to have in order to be successful. I've had many days where I was DOWN over $1,000, but I had conviction in the trade based on what I saw on the charts, so I kept the trade open, and eventually it came back in my favor and I made money.

The point is: when you scale up, you will see BIG numbers, sometimes red. You must be psychologically ready to handle it without freaking out. If you're scared of seeing some red on your P&L, the career of day trading has some harsh realities in store for you. That's why I'll say this over and over: DO NOT scale up until you're *truly* ready. Nobody else can tell you when this will be, so this is a 'come to Jesus' moment you'll need to have with yourself, if and when you get to that point.

When you DO feel you're ready to scale up, do it SLOWLY. Go from 3-5 contracts to 10 contracts per day. Do that for *a long time.* Once a 10 contract day feels very comfortable, then try 15 contracts per day. Again, do that for a long time. Do not jump from 3 contracts per day to 20, even if you have the funds for it. What works for 3 contracts won't work the same way for 20 and trading 20 contracts per day won't work the same as trading 100 contracts per day.

CHAPTER 19

Money Money Money

"Too many people spend money they earned...to buy things
they don't want...to impress people that they don't like."

—Will Rogers

The content of this entire book has been about how to make
money by day trading stock options. Notice I said *the content*
of the book is about making money by day trading. The
content is not the *meaning*. The meaning of it all is something
that each and every one of you will need to determine for
yourselves.

The HOW of something is not always the WHY of it. For all
of us who do this every day, the *how* is— we day trade, and
we make money doing it. For me, the *why* of it is personal
freedom, extra time, a sense of personal accomplishment
from teaching myself how to do something so extraordinary.
I could have an extra $1,000 in the bank, or an extra
$100,000... it doesn't really matter. The money is the means
for me to be able to do all of the things in life I want to do,
but it's not the ends. The money is not my 'why' of it.

And there's nothing wrong if the money IS your 'why' of it. Perhaps money is the most important thing in the world to you, and you like to take selfies holding up stacks of hundred dollar bills and swim in huge piles of cash like Scrooge McDuck. Cool, I'm not going to kink shame you. Each of us has our own personal level of importance we assign to money in and of itself.

This chapter is all about giving money the proper amount of respect. And when I say 'giving money the proper amount of respect' what I mean is—decide how important money is to *you* and respect it accordingly. Fine-tune your own personal trading style to align with your level of respect. Being a fairly radical life-long punk rocker, I probably value money differently than a lot of other people do. You could say I have more in common with Elliot Alderson than Gordon Gekko, and that attitude comes with it's own set of pros and cons.

On the pros side:

- I don't stress too hard or lose sleep over my losses

- I don't get hung up on making a certain amount of income every day—green is green

- I'm OK with taking a larger amount of risk on a daily basis because I'm not afraid of losing

- My larger risk tolerance allows me to make bigger gains when I'm winning because I 'let it ride' longer when I'm winning

But there are some cons too:

- That extra tolerance for risk can result in larger losses when things don't go my way

- Sometimes I hold positions open for too long when I should have stopped out sooner

- Sometimes I don't take profits as quickly as I should have, because I'm not counting every penny of income

So hopefully you can see how the differences in how you personally respect money will alter the way you trade, and what type of risk you're willing to accept as the trade is open.

I do believe that a moderate, 'middle of the road' approach to money is ultimately the smartest option for most people. You don't want to be so conservative that you never let yourself swing for the fences, but at the same time you don't want to be so freewheeling that you're going all-in on every trade.

NO GREED, NO FEAR

Read the above statement. Read it again. Internalize it. Practice it every day as you trade. GREED and FEAR are two emotions you should eliminate from your process. They are both extremely detrimental to your trading. Remember:

1. Never be afraid to lose money

2. Never let greed hinder your ability to walk away

If you're seeing the charts correctly, and if you're interpreting the information correctly, then you'll come to a well-informed decision about WHY it's good to go long or short at a particular time. And when you do this, logic is on your side. DO NOT be afraid to take the trade because of whatever irrational fear, or 'gut feeling' or any other excuse you come up with in your mind. Buy the ticket, take the ride. Don't let your fear keep you from your own success.

And just like you shouldn't be afraid to *take* the trade, don't be afraid to *get out* of a trade simply because you want to squeeze out a few more dollars' profit, or hold on a bit longer (*if you're losing*) to make back your losses. **Don't let the power of greed creep into your mind.**

If the chart tells you that you can stay in a bit longer, then stay in longer. But when the chart says it's time to cash out, DO NOT stay in longer than you should. If price action is straddling the edge of a reversal and you've already made $295, do not think, *"I just want to crack $300 today"* even when the chart is telling you it's getting very dangerous to stay in the trade. Get out and enjoy your $295. That's $295 dollars you didn't have 30 minutes earlier.

And more often than not, if you DO stay in longer than you should, before you know it, your $295 is suddenly $240 or less. In hindsight, you'll see it's MUCH better to get out with your $295 than hold on and watch your gains slowly evaporate, and then finally close it when they're down in the double digits. Green is green. First, be happy with your gains, and *then* think about how to make those gains even bigger tomorrow.

Successful trading involves the complete mastery of your own thoughts and emotions. Just like Martial Artists train their bodies with specific repetitive movements and physical exercises, trading is a mental exercise that allows us to become a better version of ourselves daily, and that's one of the many reasons I love doing it. If you've been an accountant for 30 years, do you really think that one day you'll walk into your office and have some 'lightbulb moment' that allows you to do somebody's taxes 100% better than you could do them yesterday?

With day trading, there is an opportunity to make radical advances in what you understand about it and how you do it, every single day. At this point in my career I'm basically set in my ways because I have a fully developed, fine-tuned strategy that gets results. But once in a while even I will notice a particular thing on a chart, or I'll see some new pattern emerge, and I'll think to myself, *"Wow, I never noticed that before!"* And that's a pretty amazing thing to have happen, even years into it.

DO NOT LET YOUR JOB BECOME YOUR LIFE

Before going full time with day trading, I worked for over a decade in the advertising business, first as a copywriter, then as an Associate Creative Director, then as a Creative Director. I worked at many different agencies ranging in size, from dozens to thousands of people on staff. And no matter what country I was living in, or the size of the agency, or the size of the clients I was working for, there was one thing that I ALWAYS observed in every situation—creatives feeling disgruntled and unfulfilled at work.

And what was the reason? They had allowed their jobs to become their main source of creative satisfaction. And what I mean specifically is: they inextricably linked their own sense of 'creative fulfillment' in *life* with the creative fulfillment they got from their *work*... and that is the first mistake you can make whenever you have a 'creative' job.

The thing is—in advertising *(and I'm sure in many other arts-related jobs)*, there will always be some dumb-ass client who thinks they're a better copywriter than the copywriter at the agency, or they think they've got a snazzier idea for the art direction. If you've ever worked in advertising, I don't even need to explain these to you: *"Can you make the logo bigger?"*

Or, *"I'm not exactly sure how to explain what I'm looking for… but I'll know it when I see it!"*

You will NEVER find true, artistic, creative fulfillment if you're only seeking it through your work efforts. And this is why I never had the problem of experiencing 'creative angst' at work… because I never *expected* work to give me any type of true creative fulfillment. I simply found that fulfillment elsewhere, on my own time. My approach to work was professional, but realistic. I would think about my job like this: I'm renting my brain out to the agency for a certain amount of hours every day, for a certain amount of money — and during that time I'll do my best at *giving them what they want*. it's not about what I want. I'll go do what *I want to do* when I'm finished working.

The creative 'me time' happened after work, when I would write/record/perform music, or do photography or creative writing. I was able to separate the idea of *work creativity* with *personal creativity*. So what's the point of this story, and how does it relate to day trading? The point I'm trying to make is: **never let your job become your life, even when your job is day trading.**

A lot of traders fall into this trap by failing to disconnect from the charts and the news, and by 'checking in' to see what's happening in the markets throughout the day, even when they're finished trading. I don't do this. When I'm finished trading for the day, I'm DONE with all financial matters until the next morning. I don't turn on CNBC in the afternoon, I don't open new trades in the afternoon, I don't even look at what's happening in the market—none of it.

When I close my last position at whatever time it is in the morning, I shut down TOS and then I'm doing my own thing for the rest of the day. The only time I'm still watching my screens past 9:30-10AM is on those rare days when the trade doesn't work out at first, but I haven't closed the position because my technical analysis tells me it's in my best interest to keep it open a bit longer. Those days do happen occasionally.

Remember, the 'in 5 hours per week' part of this strategy only works if you let it work. And if you sit in front of your screens watching price action all day even after you've closed your last position, you're essentially working for free. Of course, you'll *need* to do this when you're starting out *(it's a bit like taking an unpaid internship)*... but once you know what you're doing and you're actually making a living doing this, time is money—so maximize both by focusing intensely on the trade every second you're in it, but then step away and enjoy everything else you want to do in life when you've closed your last position for the day.

You can always make back the money you've lost, but you can never make back the time you've spent.

CHAPTER 20

Remember What's Truly Valuable

"You are—your life, and nothing else."—Jean-Paul Sartre

I want to start this last chapter by sharing a story that permanently impacted the way I experience life itself. This might seem like it has nothing to do with money—but it does have everything to do with realizing how important it is to be grateful for everything you have...and that in itself is an attitude that can give you more *true* wealth than anything else in the world.

Many years ago when I was still working in the advertising business, I was at an ad agency called BBDO in Manilla, Philippines. One day, I was taking a road tip from Manila up into the surrounding mountains with a few of the guys I worked with. As we cruised along the highway we passed by a gigantic landfill. I mean *gigantic*. It was an extremely hot day *(like most days in the Philippines)* and I can still remember the incredible stench wafting from the seemingly endless mountains of garbage, piled up as far as the eye could see into the horizon.

I found out from my friends that these were referred to as trash cities. I said, *"Why are they called trash cities and not just garbage dumps?"* And then I saw a bunch of children playing amongst the garbage. I asked with astonishment, *"What are those kids doing there?"* My friends informed me that those kids LIVED THERE. In fact, entire families lived there. That's why they're called trash *cities.* People with nowhere else to go literally built their shelters from the garbage they found right there in the landfill. A city built *from* trash, *in* trash. I was immediately overwhelmed with emotion. The sheer heaviness of it was absolutely heartbreaking, and I wondered how this type of reality could exist anywhere besides an active war zone.

But then I noticed something I never would have predicted in a million years. The kids were smiling, laughing, playing with each other. Looking very much like any kids at any playground anywhere. I couldn't believe it. How was this possible? That singular moment completely blew my mind wide open and changed the way I thought, forever.

I'm definitely NOT telling this story to suggest anything like, *"See, you can overcome whatever you set your mind to!"* or, *"Even if you're poor it's no big deal"* or to make light of their experience. The fact that ANYONE has to live in garbage is a tragedy and a complete failure of modern society, full stop. There's no other way to put it. The point I'm trying to make is—if those kids could smile and play and actually be happy in *those* conditions... what could *possibly* make me feel like *my* life is unfair? At that moment, I vowed to forever change the way I interpreted the experience of my own life.

After seeing this, I reflected on the way I had dealt with many of the people in my life up until that point, and I realized in hindsight that I had definitely acted selfish or entitled in many situations. I saw too many things from my own myopic perspective, feeling sorry for myself when I had no right to... things like that. After I saw those kids, at that exact moment I said to myself, *"I will NEVER feel sorry for myself about ANYTHING, ever again."* And I haven't. Not for one second, no matter what's happened to me since then.

So why am I bringing this up, and what does it have to do with day trading? It's to remind you to keep everything in perspective, and to realize how lucky you are to even have the chance to attempt this. Remember how I said optimism is essential? I also believe gratitude is essential. When you can *truly* appreciate everything you have in life, you're far less likely to say, *"I need MORE"* constantly.

So whenever you *think* you've had a hard day, or you say to yourself, *"This is SO unfair! The market made me lose $80 today"*... just STFU and ask yourself how you'd do living in a trash city. Is it really so tragic that you don't have an extra $900 stashed away for a brand new iPhone? Are you going to lament the fact that you only made $100 on the day instead of $400? The fact is: if you have thousands of dollars in a trading account, and you're able to trade the stock market every day, you're *already* winning.

There's no reason for me not to feel absolutely grateful EVERY single day I'm alive. I make a healthy six-figure yearly income. I do it in 5 hours *(or less)* per week. And I do it without having to deal with a single living person. *That*, my friends, is my absolute definition of a dream job.

I can spend my entire work day in my bathrobe if I feel like it. If I wanted to live in Sydney, Australia and start my work day at 11:30 PM, I could do it. I could work from lower Manhattan or the Nebraska panhandle. There is literally no other profession in existence that gives you this amount of freedom. It is truly the freest job you will ever have, if you stick with it and make it work for you.

So here we are at the end of the book, and now I'm going to take you back to the very beginning. If you were paying attention, you'll realize I gave away the ending of the story back at the introduction:

"It became obvious just how important it was for me to create my own reality, design my own life exactly as I want to live it, and then do whatever it took to build that life—so that's what I did."

When you're old and on your deathbed, and you think back on your life, will you think to yourself, *"I remember back when I got the newest VR headset on the day it came out."* NO, you will not.

Me? I'll remember resting my head on my dad's shoulder when I was about 5 years old, as he held me in his arms and danced around our living room while listening to Beethoven and Bach and Mozart. I'll remember helping him build giant steel sculptures using the crane on the back of his decommissioned fire truck. I'll remember the feeling of walking into the legendary CBGB's when my band played there for the first time, on my 21st birthday. I'll remember training at many different Muay Thai camps in Thailand, and the strong smell of liniment oil in the air, and the sound of the fighters' kicks reverberating like gunshots across the gym every time their shins hit the kick pads. I'll remember how it felt to float in the ocean, gazing at lush green mountains in the distance as massive waves crashed over my head, while experiencing one of those fabled 'one with nature' moments.

There are many more things I'll remember—and none of them involve objects that can be bought with money.

And that leads me to the singular most important concept in this whole book:

I do not trade to gain MONEY. I trade to gain FREEDOM.

Following the herd is what keeps you addicted to owning the latest and greatest commodities, which keeps you beholden to making a certain amount of money. You need the latest car/phone/watch/handbag/wardrobe for *what*, exactly? Is it really you, *truly* the "real you" who needs these things, or is it your addiction to being part of the herd that makes you need these things?

Lone Wolves don't need a pack. They don't need to impress anyone, and they don't need to *belong* to anyone or anything.

Trading is simply the way I make my money, and making all of my money in 5 hours per week is the way I make freedom. THAT is absolutely the BEST thing about doing this for a living.

Thank you for reading this book. I hope you will now go forth, trade well, and create whatever type of life you envision for yourself.

About the author

Patrick Buchanan is a writer, musician, photographer, filmmaker and citizen of the world. He's lived on 3 continents and visited over 30 countries, and currently splits his time between the US, South America and South East Asia. When he's not making his living day trading, he conducts private online coaching sessions to teach traders his strategy 1 on 1. In his free time, he writes and records music, tours with various bands, trains in the martial art of Muay Thai, and creates fine art and fashion photography. Visit his website at www.lonewolftradingclub.com for more info.

Get in touch!

Feel free to contact me anytime and follow me on social media. On my website you can find my complete, 7+ hour options day trading video course. I am also available for 1-on-1 or group coaching sessions and for speaking engagements at conferences.

Website: www.lonewolftradingclub.com

Email: lonewolftradingclub@gmail.com

YouTube: @LoneWolfTradingClub

Instagram: @lonewolftradingclub

X: @LoneWolfTrader0

Printed in Great Britain
by Amazon

41972485R00175